The **Answer** Book

answrs.co

Text written by Clifford Goldstein
Media content provided by It Is Written
Cover and Layout Design by Robert Koorenny
Style edited by Lauren Lascon
Copy edited by Arlene Clark

Type set: 11.5pt Avenir Next

Image credits:
© Eric Tirado: page 63
© Robert Koorenny: pages 59, 70
Images with no credit are used under Public Domain or do not require attribution

Published by Typo Fire, www.typofire.com
Printed in the U.S.A.

ISBN 13: 978-0-9851702-4-0

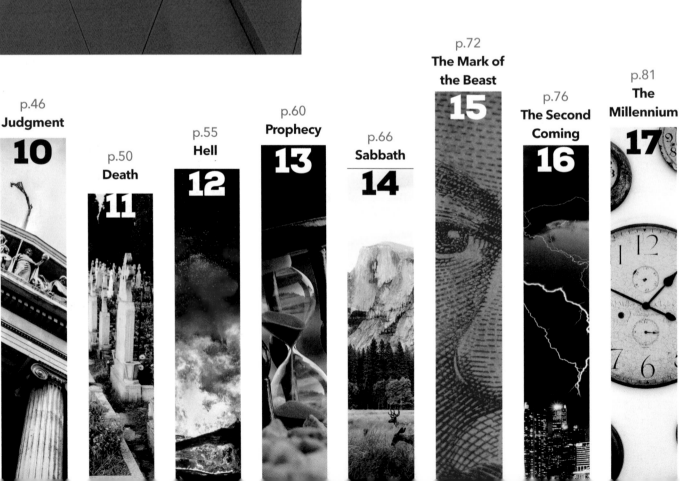

Connect with us!

@theanswerbook
instagram.com/theanswerbook

@bibleanswerbook
fb.me/bibleanswerbook

www.answrs.co

Topics

INTRODUCTION

Don't Nobody Know Why

A young man, newly-married, had survived the atomic bombing of Hiroshima. Not so his bride: nothing remained of this young lady, so full of life, love, and enthusiasm but charred bones, which he—desperate to bring to her parents—gathered into a small covered bowl. Then, amid the chaos, he managed to get out of Hiroshima, the bowl of bones snug in his arms as he caught a train to the city where her parents lived.

That city, however, was Nagasaki, where days later a second atomic bomb was dropped. Yes, this man was one of the rare people to have been nuked not once but twice and, even rarer, to have survived both. However, just as the first blast turned his wife to bones, the second blew open the top of the bowl and these bones vanished forever from his reach.

"All this way! All this way," he cried out, "and her bones are scattered who knows where—and to what purpose?"

Good question, is it not? All this way, all this way, and to what purpose? Sometimes life itself—without the drama of being nuked (twice!)—can make us wonder for what purpose is it all. We live, we suffer, and sooner or later we die, and everyone who ever knew us dies … and on it goes, generation after generation after generation. The pain and suffering that follow us like our shadows, as deep as our souls and as constant as breath, can make it all seem so futile.

Just Set Down Here

"Seem like we're just set down here," an old lady lamented, "and don't nobody know why."

Just set down here, and don't nobody know why?

Though not exactly expressed in King's English, this quote does catch the human dilemma. We were brought into existence without our consent, given a whole set of circumstances (parents, date of birth, place of birth, eye color, etc.) that we didn't chose, and, in most cases, we die neither in a time, place, or manner of our own choosing as well.

Just set down here, and don't nobody know why?

Maybe, but that hasn't stopped some people from guessing why. Ancient cultures had all sorts of creation stories—everything from a cosmic egg being the origin of life, to one god spitting on the ground and creating humans with his spit, to the universe always existing, to a turtle carrying mud on its back until eventually making the earth.

Today, the moderns have their own creation stories to explain why were "just set down here" as well. Peter Atkins, a British chemist, argued that nothing created us. And when he says "nothing," he means nothing, as in not-a-thing at all. "From now on", he writes, "by nothing I shall mean absolutely nothing. I shall mean less than empty space. … This Nothing has no space and no time. This Nothing is absolutely nothing. A void devoid of space and time. Utter emptiness. Emptiness beyond emptiness. All that it has, is a name."

Dr. Atkins then states his goal: "I want to show that Nothing is the foundation of everything."

Francis Crick, one of the greatest scientists in the twentieth century, believed that space aliens from another planet seeded life on earth, and that's how we were "just set down here."

Meanwhile, sounding like the *Return of the Jedi* meets *The Matrix*, one philosopher argued that we don't even really exist, but are computer algorithms created by a race of super-aliens using high-powered Macs or the like. "There is a significant probability," wrote Nick Bostrum, "that you are living in [a] computer simulation. I mean this literally: if the simulation argument is true, you exist in a virtual reality simulated in a computer built by some advanced civilization."

Even if Bostrum were right and we don't exist, we sure feel as if we do, and so we're still stuck with the tough questions of how to make the best of whatever we are and however it was that we were "just set down here."

Mourning Birth

But that's not always easy to do, is it? A Greek historian who lived more than 2400 years ago told about a tribe of people who, when a baby came into the world, sat around mourning because they knew the troubles that this baby, if it even survived, would face as an adult. That's not how we treat the arrival of a newborn in our culture, for sure, but one can't really argue with their logic, can we?

"I cried when I was born," wrote poet George Herbert, "and every day shows why."

Pain, struggle, disappointment, who doesn't know it (lots of it, too)? And even if we don't know a lot of it ourselves, how can we live with the realization of all the suffering that goes on around us?

An Austrian Jew who had fled the Nazi's, Stephen Zweig wrote: "I realized that all the time one was laughing and cracking silly jokes, somewhere in the world someone was lying at the point of death; that misery was lurking, people starving, behind a thousand windows; that there were such things as hospitals, quarries and coalmines; that in factories, in offices, in prisons countless thousands toiled and moiled at every hour of the day, and that it would not relieve the distress of a single human being if yet another were to torment himself needlessly. Were one to attempt, I was quite certain, to visualize the misery that existed at any one time all over the world, there would be an end of one's sleep and the smiles would die on one's lips."

In his Vietnam War memoir, American Philip Caputo wrote about responding to John Fitzgerald Kennedy's call to "Ask not what your country can do for you, but what you can do for your country." He thought he could do something for his country by fighting in Vietnam. Yet, before long, officers were offering the soldiers beer for every enemy combatant whom they killed. "That is the level to which we had sunk from the lofty idealism of a year before," he wrote. "We were going to kill people for a few cans of beer and the time off to drink it."

And, as if life itself weren't hard enough, what about death? Whether sitting in a synagogue in Pennsylvania and getting shot, or sitting in your office at the World Trade Center and being hit by a hijacked jetliner filled with people, we can—in an instant—be wiped out.

The saying goes, "You can't avoid death and taxes." Wrong. There have been plenty of tax cheats, but death cheats? Good luck with that. Sure, some things are worse than death, but whatever they are they must be pretty bad when death is deemed better.

American author Annie Dillard wrote about the time her father "tried to explain why men on Wall Street had jumped from skyscrapers when the stock market crashed: 'They lost everything!'—but of course I thought they lost everything only when they jumped."

Or, what about the world's most famous athe-

WELCOME

visit **answrs.co/welcome** to meet Pastor John Bradshaw and learn how to connect and use the resources found in this book.

ist, Dr. Richard Dawkins? He wrote about fellow biologist, D.W. Hamilton, who had requested that his corpse be interred in the Amazon jungle with a bunch of beetles, which he apparently liked to study. Dawkin's quoted Hamilton's wife's eulogy at the funeral, which took place in England instead of the Amazon, as he had wanted. She said: "Bill, now your body is lying in the Wytham woods, but from here you will reach again your beloved forests. You will live not only in a beetle, but in billions of spores of fungi and algae. Brought by the wind higher up in the troposphere, all of you will form the clouds, and wandering across oceans, will fall down and fly up again and again, till eventually a drop of rain will join you to the water of the flooded forest of the Amazon."

Floating around in spores of fungi and algae? Not the most thrilling of prospects, or the most glorious ending to a human existence, is it? But what else can Dr. Dawkins offer us, or anyone, in a world where death alone solves the dilemma of human suffering?

Making Sense of Nonsense?

How does one make sense of all this? How does one make sense of so much that, in and of itself, seems nonsensical? These are not easy questions to answer, and people have been struggling with them from the days of old.

Now, in the midst of all this madness, one man in history, more than anyone else, claimed to have answers. Not just claimed to have answers. No, He claimed much more than that.

He claimed to be the answer.

And that man was Jesus Christ, a Jewish preacher from ancient Judea, which, at the time of Jesus, was a backwater province of the great Roman Empire. And this Jesus made the kind of claims about Himself that don't allow for a middle ground regarding His identity.

He said, for instance: "I am the way, the truth, and the life. No one comes to the Father except through Me" (John 14:6). Or: "I am the resurrection and the life. He who believes in Me, though he may die, he shall live" (John 11:25). Or: "You search the Scriptures, for in them you think you have eternal life; and these are they which testify of Me" (John 5:39).

Sorry, folks, but a good man, a prophet of God, a faithful Jew will not make these claims about Himself unless they were true. Either Jesus was a nut case, a lunatic, a great deceiver; or He was who He claimed to be and what others in the Bible said He was: God Himself having come to earth in human flesh.

This book, which you hold in your hand, accepts the latter conclusion: that Jesus of Nazareth was, indeed, God and, as such, He is the answer to the hard questions of life. This book will look at the Scriptures "which testify of me", Jesus said. What does the Bible testify about Jesus? About the meaning of life? About the meaning of death? About the past, the present, the future? Who are we, actually? Why are we here? How will the world end?

In the 1700s a German writer asked three basic questions: What can I know? What should I do? What can I hope for? All these answers, and more, are found in the Word of God and in Jesus Christ.

"Seem like we're just set down here, and don't nobody know why." Not quite. We're weren't just set down here. We were created by God, a loving God, for a reason. In Jesus and in His Word we can know the reason, we can "know why". We can have answers to the hard questions, and we can have a hope that transcends even the most painful of answers.

01

THE WORD OF GOD

The User Manual

In the 1950s, a conductor was walking through a train in New Jersey checking tickets when he was stunned to find himself face-to-face with the famous Dr. Albert Einstein. Einstein reached into his pocket but couldn't find his ticket. He frantically dug around until the conductor told him not to worry about it and moved on. Later, when the conductor was walking back through the train, he saw Einstein, on his knees, looking for the ticket on the floor.

"Dr. Einstein," he said, "I told you that I trust you bought the ticket for where you're going. You don't need to find it."

Einstein looked up and said, "I need to find it because I don't know where I am going."

Says something, doesn't it? If Albert Einstein, one of the greatest geniuses of all time, didn't know where he was going, what about the rest of us mere mortals? Where are we going? What are we doing here? What is the purpose of our lives?

The good news is that we can find answers—that the God who created us, who put us here, didn't just plop us down and say, *You're on your own, kiddos*. On the contrary, questions about who we are, why we are here, how we are to live, where we are going are so important that God didn't leave it up to us to try and find the answers on our own.

No, the answers to these questions are so important that God revealed them to us in the Scriptures, also known as the Word of God.

Here I Stand

One of the most famous and consequential moments in all of Western history occurred in the German town of Worms in 1521. A single German monk, Martin Luther, stood up against the power of the Roman Church, which for a thousand years dominated ecclesiastical, and to some degree political, life in Europe, and before whom popes, kings, and princes trembled. And now, condemned, damned, excommunicated, vilified, and deemed an enemy of God, of truth, of heaven, and pretty much all else, this one man, alone, stood before a tribunal of some of Europe's most powerful personages, including the emperor, Charles V. It was there, before this august body, that Luther was ordered to recant his teachings, which had reverberated through the European continent—teachings that were to become the foundation of the Protestant Reformation.

WATCH visit **answrs.co/ bible** to see a short video on the Word of God | 2:40

The Holy Bible

Written...
by more than 40 authors
over a span of about 1,500 years
on three different continents
in three languages

The Old Testament   The New Testament

The Old Testament	The New Testament
39 books	27 books
23,145 verses	7,957 verses
Written in Hebrew and Aramaic	Written in Koine Greek

Harangued, threatened, disparaged, and under intense pressure to back off, Luther refused, claiming that his position rested on the one sure foundation, the Bible. Thus, before a powerful group of men, many who wanted nothing more than him dead (this was a time where religious deviation could mean getting burned at the stake), Luther uttered these famous lines:

"Since your most serene majesty and the princes require a simple, clear, and direct answer, I will give one, and it is this: I cannot submit my faith either to the pope or to the councils, because it is as clear as noonday that they have often fallen into error, and even into glaring inconsistency with themselves. If, then, I am not convinced by proof from Holy Scripture, or by cogent reasons; if I am not satisfied by the very texts that I have cited, and if my judgment is not in this way brought into subjection to God's Word, I neither can nor will retract anything; for it cannot be right for a Christian to speak against his conscience. Here I take my stand; I cannot do otherwise. God be my help! Amen."

In other words, on the Bible Martin Luther was willing to stake his life—and history has never been the same since.

What Is This Book?

What is this book, then, that is so radically unlike any other book in history? What is this ancient text, in some sections more than 3,000 years old, that is loved and revered by so many, even today, and yet hated and denigrated by so many, even today? What is this book, over which wars have been waged, revolutions started, and kingdoms brought to dust? What is this book that some have been willing to die for and others, unfortunately, to kill for? What is the Bible?

To put it in the simplest terms possible, the Bible is God's instruction manual for humanity. Think about it. Babies aren't born with instructions, are they? It just doesn't work that way. Who we are, why we are here, how we are to live, what happens when we die, what is the purpose of our

BIBLE FACT
More than 5,000,000,000 copies of the Bible have been sold.

existence—the answers to these questions are not written in the stars (though some look there for answers). They're not etched in the clouds, echoed in the wind, or sung in the sounds of ocean waves.

No, that is why the God who created us, who put us here, has given us the Bible, which has the answers we crave. Again, because these are such significant questions, and it's so important that we get them right—instead of us being left to try and figure them out on our own God answered them for us in the Bible.

When you buy a new product, the user manual often comes in the package, written by the people who thought up the product, created it, know exactly what its purpose is, and know how best to use it. It's kind of like that with Scripture: It was inspired by God, the One who thought us up, created us, sustains us, loves us, and knows what's best for us.

History of God in the World

On the other hand, like all analogies, the user manual one has limits, because Scripture is so much more than just a user manual. Aside from teaching us who we are, how we got here, and where we are going, the Bible is also the story of God's interaction with humanity. Through that interaction God has provided us with the answers to these important questions. From the opening verses to the last verses, the Scriptures reveal God's working in our world. Although some people teach the theory that God created the world and then left

WATCH
visit **answrs.co/trust** to watch *Can God be Trusted?* | 58:30

it on its own, the Bible shows God's close and intimate interaction with humanity. Through the biblical accounts of these interactions, crucial truths are revealed to us—truths that we could never figure out by ourselves.

Search the Scriptures

In the New Testament, a scene unfolds where Jesus of Nazareth, in a confrontation with the religious leaders, makes the following claim: "You search the Scriptures, for in them you think you have eternal life; and these are they which testify of Me" (John 5:39).

There's no question that these men revered the Scripture, which was good. However, they revered it so much that they thought they could find eternal life in the Scripture itself, which was bad. Jesus told them that life—eternal life—didn't come from the Bible itself, as if something mystical happened by interaction with the texts, but only from the God revealed in those texts. The Bible is not the end in itself but the means to the end—that end is our Creator, Maker, and Redeemer.

Our Creator, Maker, and Redeemer is Jesus Christ, whose greatest and most intimate interaction with humanity was to take upon Himself our human body, our flesh and blood, and live among us as one of us. Talk about intimacy! Thus, from the creation of this world (Genesis 1) to the creation of a new

LISTEN IN visit **answrs.co/word** to listen to a presentation that goes along with what you're reading in this chapter.

Q&A FROM THE BIBLE

What is another name for the Bible?
"But Jesus answered him, saying, 'It is written, Man shall not live by bread alone, but by every **word of God**'" (Luke 4:4).

"Jesus said to them, 'Have you never read in the **Scriptures**?'" (Matthew 21:42).

How did we receive the Scripture?
"All Scripture is given by **inspiration of God**, and is profitable for doctrine, for reproof, for correction, for instruction in righteousness" (2 Timothy 3:16).

How did God inspire individuals to write His Word?
"For prophecy never came by the will of man, but holy men of God spoke as they were **moved by the Holy Spirit**" (2 Peter 1:21).

How much of the Bible is beneficial for us?
"**All Scripture** is given by inspiration of God, and is profitable for doctrine, for reproof, for correction, for instruction in righteousness, 17 that the man of God may be complete, thoroughly equipped for every good work" (2 Timothy 3:16, 17).

What should I ask for so that I can understand the Bible?
"It is written in the prophets, 'And they shall all be **taught by God**'" (John 6:45).

"But the **Helper**, the **Holy Spirit**, whom the Father will send in My name, **He will teach you** all things, and bring to your remembrance all things that I said to you" (John 14:26).

"If you then, being evil, know how to give good gifts to your children, how much more will your heavenly Father **give the Holy Spirit to those who ask Him**!" (Luke 11:13).

"**Open my eyes**, that I may see wondrous things from Your law" (Psalm 119:18).

How often should I spend time reading and thinking about God's word?
"This Book of the Law shall not depart from your mouth, but you shall meditate in it **day and night**, that you may observe to do according

one (Revelation 21:1), the Bible is the story of God's great love for humanity, especially as it is revealed in the life and death of Jesus Christ.

Self-Authenticating

Q&A: The Word of God

WATCH visit **answrs.co/true** to watch a video answering questions including *How can you believe Christianity is true?* and *How do we know the Bible hasn't changed?*

All this, however, leads to a fair question: Why should someone believe the Bible? Christians often say that we have to take it on faith, and that's true, but it is not a blind faith.

On the contrary, the Bible itself gives us powerful and compelling reasons to believe what it teaches. From the amazing fulfillments of prophecy, particularly those prophecies pointing to Jesus many centuries before He came, to the prophecies about world history, to what it teaches about history, to the book's amazing unity (after all, it was written by dozens of people, in some cases separated by more than a thousand years from each other), to what it teaches about creation, to the lives changed by it—the Bible gives us compelling reasons for trusting it as the Word of God.

Anyone who approaches the Bible with an open and honest mind—that is, neither a hard to all that is written in it. For then you will make your way prosperous, and then you will have good success" (Joshua 1:8).

What grows stronger as I spend time reading and thinking about God's Word?
"So then **faith** comes by hearing, and hearing by the word of God" (Romans 10:17).

Is faith essential for the Christian?
"For by grace you have been **saved through faith**" (Ephesians 2:8).

"But **without faith it is impossible to please Him**, for he who comes to God must believe that He is, and that He is a rewarder of those who diligently seek Him" (Hebrews 11:6).

What did Jesus say Scripture speaks about?
"You search the Scriptures, for in them you think you have eternal life; and these are they which **testify of Me**" (John 5:39).

What happens if I spend time in the Bible?
"having been **born again**, not of corruptible seed but incorruptible, through the word of God which lives and abides forever" (1 Peter 1:23).

"that He might sanctify and **cleanse** her with the **washing of water by the word**" (Ephesians 5:26).

How does memorizing the Bible help me?
"Your word I have hidden in my heart, that I **might not sin** against You" (Psalm 119:11).

What does reading the Bible give us?
"For whatever things were written before were written for our learning, that we through the patience and **comfort of the Scriptures** might have **hope**" (Romans 15:4).

What is the Bible full of that brings comfort and hope?
"By which have been given to us **exceedingly great** and **precious promises**, that through these you may be partakers of the divine nature, having escaped the corruption that is in the world through lust" (2 Peter 1:14).

Will these promises ever fail us?
"So shall my word be that goes out from my mouth; it shall **not return** to me **empty**, but it shall **accomplish** that which I purpose, and shall **succeed** in the thing for which I sent it" (Isaiah 55:11, ESV).

heart determined not to believe, *no matter the evidence*; or a naïve gullibility ready to accept anything, *no matter how silly*—that person can find powerful evidence for belief.

Personal Experience

In a story mocking Christianity, a robot had been designed to do a person's believing for them; that is, the robot supposedly expressed faith so that its owner didn't need to. That story misses the point. We all express faith, and all the time, too—even in earthly and mundane things that we don't fully understand (will the car start, will the medicine work, will the weather report hold true?). If we trust in things of this world that

we can't fully comprehend, how much more should we trust in things of a divine and heavenly nature?

But the good news about the Christian faith, as revealed in the Bible, is that we are given good reasons for believing in Jesus Christ and what He did for humanity. In Him, we can find answers—hopeful and wonderful answers—to the tough questions about life, answers that even Einstein couldn't find on his own.

Ancient scrolls DISCOVERED in forgotten caves

Giving Light to Our World

READ MORE + SHARE THIS TOPIC
Visit **www.glowonline.org/answer/scrolls** to read more about what you just read here. You can also share it on social media.

02

THE ORIGIN OF LIFE

White Stuff

Imagine (momentarily) that you lived on another planet, and that on this planet all your food had always been created in factories only. That's all you had ever experienced—food in cans and boxes coming out of massive industrial plants like widgets off an assembly line.

Suppose, though, that you heard about another planet where someone would take a pellet made of white stuff and stick it in ground. Then, over time, with water and sunshine, a massive trunk of inedible matter, called "wood," would grow out of this tiny pellet of white stuff and, on that trunk, many branches of more wood would grow. But, then, on each of these inedible branches, packets of the most wonderful and tasty food, called "grapefruit," would slowly appear—each one covered a thick skin that protected the food inside.

And suppose you were told that each grapefruit contained more pellets of white stuff just like what it had originated from. That is, the white stuff, when mixed with water and dirt and sunshine, would create copies of itself. And suppose you were told that this newly created white stuff in each new grapefruit—when mixed with dirt and water and sunshine—will create another inedible trunk of wood sprouting more branches of inedible wood, from which more self-contained packets of fruit would grow, each one containing more pellets of white stuff that, too, mixed with water, dirt, and sunshine would create more and more, and on and on ... potentially forever. *All this*, you were told, *from one pellet of white stuff?*

Why would you, why *should* you, believe it? And, even more fanciful than this story—suppose you were told that on this same planet, other pellets of varying size and textures (some so small that you can barely see them), when put in the dirt with water and sunshine, created all sorts of other incredibly beautiful and tasty food that contained more self-replicating pellets of their own kind?

Why would you believe what sounds like science fiction? Or, even if you did believe it—would you not deem these pellets miraculous?

We Are Here

For us, these "miraculous" pellets are—what? Seeds. Big deal! Yet, it seems like no big deal to us because we're so used to what seeds do; we've become hardened to how miraculous they really are.

This is how many of us approach all life on Earth. We just take it for granted, not always realizing that, however we got here, *it's a miracle that we are here*. Amid an airless and harsh cosmos filled with exploding stars, temperature extremes, asteroids, radiation, black holes, cosmic dust, and colliding galaxies all so inhospitable to life—here we are, anyway.

Scientists talk about the incredible balance of cosmic and atomic forces: just the right amount of this, just the right amount of that—otherwise life as we know it could not exist. Imagine a wall with

Q&A: The Origin of Life

WATCH visit **answrs.co/created** to watch a video answering questions including *How long ago was the earth created?*, *Where do dinosaurs fit into the story of creation?* and *How do you know the earth was created in six days?*

40 dials, each dial calibrated with mind-numbing precision: in the millions, or in the billions, of settings. And if one of these dials was off by just one click–kaput! We couldn't be here. And yet, whatever the odds against us being here, we are here.

As one writer, not a Christian, expressed it, "I cannot believe that our existence in this universe is a mere quirk of fate, an accident of history. ... We are truly meant to be here."

Meant to be here? That's fine. But if that's correct, the question is: *Who, or what, meant us to be here?*

A Donkey in the Den

Imagine coming home one day and finding a donkey in your den, perhaps drinking out of the fish tank. You ask your spouse, roommate, whoever–"Where did this donkey come from?"

"The donkey came from nothing" is the reply.

That would be ridiculous, right? But if a donkey coming from nothing is ridiculous, then what about earth, the sky, the cosmos? They couldn't have come from nothing any more than a donkey could have. However, in recent years, some scientists have tried to argue that, indeed, the universe did arise from nothing. For these people, as atheists, "nothing" is their most logical explanation for creation.

Why? Because if something other than an eternally existing God had created the universe, then, whatever it was, it had to be created by something before it, which had to be created by something before it . . . and on and on endlessly into the past.

The only way to get out of this trap, called "infinite regress," is for the universe to have been created by something that, itself, was not created, and therefore needs no explanation. It seems that only two things could be viable candidates, only two things that don't themselves need explanations for their being.

The first is an eternally existing God, such as the God depicted in the Bible, because He has

WATCH visit **answrs.co/origins** to watch a video about the Biblical view of origins and life on Earth

always existed. There never was a time when He wasn't there, so He needs no explanation because He is prior to all things, including anything that could explain Him. The second is nothing. Nothing doesn't need an explanation because, after all, it is *nothing*. There is nothing there to be explained.

Peter Atkins, atheist and scientist, once said, "I want to show that nothing is the foundation of everything." Atkins and other atheist scientists take the rather strange position that nothing created the universe. They have no other choice because, well, by their ruling out an eternally existent God, their only

CREATION FACT

The sun is 400x larger than the moon, but the moon is 400x closer to the earth than the sun, which makes them appear the same size in the sky!

Q&A FROM THE BIBLE

your house.' **Immediately** he rose up before them, took up what he had been lying on, and departed to his own house, glorifying God" (Luke 5:24, 25).

How did the universe, including planet Earth and everything in it, come to exist?
"In the beginning **God created** the heavens and the earth" (Genesis 1:1).

What was the condition of our planet in the beginning?
"The earth was **without form**, and **void**; and **darkness** was on the face of the deep. And the Spirit of God was hovering over the face of the waters" (Genesis 1:2).

How did God create our planet and everything in it?
"By the word of the LORD the heavens were made, and all the host of them by the breath of His mouth … **For He spoke**, and it was done; He commanded, and it stood fast" (Psalm 33:6, 9).

"Then **God said**, 'Let there be light'; and there was light" (Genesis 1:3).

"By faith we understand that the worlds were **framed by the word of God**, so that the things which are seen were not made of things which are visible" (Hebrews 11:3).

When God speaks does His word ever fail?
"So shall My word be that goes forth from My mouth; It shall **not return to Me void**, but it shall accomplish what I please, and it shall prosper in the thing for which I sent it" (Isaiah 55:11).

How long after God speaks does it take until the thing spoken becomes real?
"As soon as He had spoken, **immediately** the leprosy left him, and he was cleansed" (Mark 1:42).

"He said to the man who was paralyzed, 'I say to you, arise, take up your bed, and go to

How long did it take to create our planet?
"For in six days the LORD made the heavens and the earth, the sea, and all that is in them, and rested the seventh day" (Exodus 20:11).

What was unique about how God created man?
"And the LORD God **formed man of the dust of the ground**, and breathed into his nostrils the breath of life; and man became a living being" (Genesis 2:7).

Which members of the three person Godhead, the Father, Son, or Spirit, actually assisted in the Creation?
"Yet for us there is one God, **the Father**, of whom are all things, and we for Him and one Lord **Jesus Christ**, through whom are all things, and through whom we live" (1 Corinthians 8:6).

"By His **Spirit** He adorned the heavens" (Job 26:13).

"And the **Spirit of God** was hovering over the face of the waters" (Genesis 1:2).

What distinguishes the true God of the Bible from the other false gods in this world?
"O LORD of hosts, God of Israel, the One who dwells between the cherubim, You are God, You alone, of all the kingdoms of the earth. **You have made heaven and earth**" (Isaiah 37:16).

"But the LORD is the true God; He is the living God and the everlasting King…Thus you shall say to them: 'The **gods** that **have not made** the heavens and the earth shall perish from the earth and from under these heavens.' **He has made the earth** by His power, He has established the world by His wisdom, and has stretched out the heavens at His discretion" (Jeremiah 10:11,12).

WATCH visit **answrs.co/ creation** to watch a short video on the topic of creation | 2:23

other option for something that doesn't itself need an explanation is, yes, nothing.

So, either an eternally existing God is responsible for the creation, or nothing is.

Take your pick.

The Creation

If you picked an eternally existing God, then you're in harmony with the Bible. Throughout Scripture a key theme is that the Lord revealed in its pages is the creator of the cosmos. The first verse of the Bible reads, "In the beginning God created the heavens and the earth" (Genesis 1:1), a theme that reoccurs all through its pages, even to the last book, Revelation. There we read, "Fear God and give glory to Him, for the hour of His judgment has come; and worship Him who made heaven and earth, the sea and springs of water" (Revelation 14:7).

In both Old Testament and New Testament, reference is made to God as the creator, which makes so much sense when we look at the beauty and the complexity of nature. If we open our eyes, reality screams out to us, not just of a creator God but of a creator of power and love.

A young man, having been an atheist all his life, had just become a Christian. As if a veil had been torn from his eyes—for the first time, he marveled at the astonishing beauty of the creation and what it said about the Creator Himself. He had been walking in a forest and, seeing the trees, the vegetation, the sunlight filtering through the leaves, a few deer, he thought: *Putting aside all theology, doctrine, denominations—I realize that whoever created all this had to be good!*

Blobs of Organized Mud

For the past few centuries, however, many have argued that all this beauty, all this complexity, is the result of chance. Evolution alone, we're assured, can explain it all without a creator—from the grapefruit seed in the grapefruit, to Beethoven writing a piano concerto. That is the claim, anyway, and because it comes under the name of "science," many uncritically accept it, not realizing how often science itself has been wrong.

One atheist evolutionist wrote the following about humanity: "We humans are blobs of organized mud." Blobs of organized mud, eh? If so, then this atheist, too, would be a blob of organized mud. How much credibility could we put in what a blob of mud—organized or not—says about anything?

This theory would mean, then, that our loves, passions, families, hopes, dreams, desires, art, music, and literature—everything—is, really, just a meaningless conglomeration of atoms and molecules and chemicals that, by chance (that is, with

LISTEN IN visit **answrs.co/life** to listen to a presentation that goes along with what you're reading in this chapter.

The Creation Week

DAY 1

God made the *Light* and divided it from the *darkness*

DAY 2

God made the *Sky* and divided it from the *water on the earth*

DAY 3

God made the *Dry land* and divided it from the *sea*, then He created *plant life*

DAY 4

God made the *Sun, Moon, and Stars*. He made the sun rule the day, and the moon rule the night

DAY 5

God made the *Animals in the water* and the *birds in the sky*

DAY 6

God made the *Animals on land* and created *man and woman* in His own image

DAY 7

Go *Reste an blessed th day calle Sabbat*

less forethought than went into baking a chocolate cake) turned into life and all that attends life! It's not just that we don't want to believe that we are only organized blobs of mud. Rather, the facts we face and our moment-by-moment reality make us realize that this position just cannot be right.

Jesus on the Cross

All right, but all this leads to a logical question. Suppose that young man who marveled at the beauty in the woods, while contemplating the wonders of nature, was mauled by a bear. Nature might be beautiful but it can be very cruel at times, too.

Yes, the same wonderful rain that brings grapefruit (and cherries, peaches, plums, wheat, tomatoes, pomegranate, and olives and on and on) can also cause a flood that kills thousands. Nature is not all sweetness and light—especially human nature, with all its evils.

How do we explain evil and suffering in light of God's love and power as revealed in His creation? That's a good question, a fair question, and it's one that this book will tackle.

But, even now we reveal a hint that points toward the answer: Jesus on the cross.

How does Jesus on the cross fit with any of this? In a big way, actually. For starters, the Bible teaches that Jesus was the One who created our world. Talking about Jesus, Scripture says that, "All things were made through Him, and without Him nothing was made that was made" (John 1:3). No, it was not from "nothing" that everything arose but, rather from Jesus, God Himself in the flesh. He is our creator.

This God, who made all that had come into existence, that is, the creator—He was the same one who, out of love for His creation, died on the cross for it. Yes, answers for the rise of evil and suffering can be found, and we will explore them in this book. But, we immediately point to Jesus, our creator, the one dying on the cross for His creation—we point to Him who not only has the answer but, indeed, is the answer. Him, Jesus Himself, our creator, sacrificing Himself for His creation, is the answer.

03

GOD THE FATHER

An Old Testament Tyrant?

Eight-year-old Stevie, born out of wedlock, never met his father. One day, he came home from school to his grandparents' house. On the upcoming Thursday, fathers were to visit the class for a "Father's Day" celebration. Stevie knew that no one was going to come for him.

"Grandma," he said, eyes downcast.

"Yes," she answered.

"Grandma," he said. "I wish that I had a daddy."

"But, Stevie," she replied, "you do have a daddy." The little boy looked up, eyes bulging with excitement, and said, "I do? I have a daddy?"

"Yes, Stevie, everyone has a daddy."

God the Father

We all have a daddy, even if in some cases he is not the man we would have chosen. In fact, none of us choose our father any more than we choose our birthday. According to the Bible, however, we all have another father, whether or not we acknowledge Him, know Him, or even believe in Him. This, of course, is God the Father.

Sure, most people know about Jesus, His life, His death, and His resurrection. Some may have also read and heard about the work of the Holy Spirit. But God the Father? Let us answer some questions about Him.

The Old Testament Tyrant?

When people think of God the Father, they think of—what? This horrible Old Testament tyrant, a God of vengeance, one who is unforgiving, unloving, and demanding utter obedience, or else—ZAP!

That view is, however, a caricature, a picture drawn from the selective misuse of some stories. This view ignores not only the context of those stories but also the big picture behind them. Far from the Father being a tyrant, the Old Testament consistently reveals a patient, loving, forgiving God who sought to bring salvation, healing, and hope to His people and, then, through them, to the whole world.

An Intimate God

Interestingly enough, perhaps the greatest Old Testament revelation about the character of the Father can be found in, well, a building. After leading the children of Israel out of Egypt, God said: "And let them make Me a sanctuary, that I may dwell among them" (Exodus 25:8).

The Creator of the universe, the God who first created all that is, from the quarks in atoms to the galaxies that span space—this God, God the Father, came to dwell among escaped slaves? It would be, to use a contemporary analogy, as if God chose to manifest His presence, in a unique way, in a refugee camp filled with displaced people who have no home to call their own.

In this manner, therefore, pray: Our Father in heaven, hallowed be Your name.

WATCH visit **answrs.co/father** to watch a short video about God the Father | 2:20

Q&A FROM THE BIBLE

Who are the different members of the Godhead?

"Therefore go and make disciples of all nations, baptizing them in the name of the **Father** and of the **Son** and of the **Holy Spirit**" (Matthew 28:19).

What is God according to the Bible?

"He who does not love does not know God, for **God is love**" (1 John 4:8).

Does the Father love us or is it just Jesus who loves us?

"For the **Father** Himself **loves** you" (John 16:27).

What has the Father done to demonstrate His love for you?

"For God so **loved the world that He gave His only begotten Son**, that whoever believes in Him should not perish but have everlasting life" (John 3:16).

"In this the **love of God was manifested** toward us, that God has **sent His only begotten Son** into the world, that we might live through Him." (1 John 4:9).

Since true love is composed of having mercy and being fair with justice how is God's character summarized?

"And he passed in front of Moses, proclaiming, "The LORD, the LORD, the **compassionate and gracious** God, **slow to anger**, abounding in **love and faithfulness**, maintaining love to thousands, and **forgiving wickedness**,

And if that weren't enough, this sanctuary was daily "polluted" by blood—the blood of animal sacrifices. This was done in order to make "atonement" for the people; that is, to make sinful fallen people right with a holy, sinless God. In other words, God the Father could have let our tiny planet, an atom in the cosmos (if even that), vanish into oblivion. But instead, He dwelt among us, a fallen race, in order to save us from disappearing forever into the nothingness out of which we first came.

A Forgiving God

In fact, time and again we find this "Old Testament tyrant" not only forgiving His people but telling them that even if they fall away from Him and receive the just consequences of their sins—He was still willing to take them back, if they would be willing to come back: "He will not forsake you nor destroy you, nor forget the covenant of your fathers which He swore to them" (Deuteronomy 4:31).

Talking about the outright evil that His people were committing, God the Father begged them to stop before it was too late, pleading: "How can I give you up, Ephraim? How can I hand you over, Israel?" (Hosea 11:8).

No wonder Isaiah the prophet wrote about God the Father this way: "For as the heavens are high above the earth, so great is His mercy toward those who fear Him; As far as the east is from the west, so far has He removed our transgressions from us. As a father pities his children, so the LORD pities those who fear Him. For He knows our frame; He remembers that we are dust" (Psalm 103:11-14).

In the rancid story of King David's affair with a military man's wife, King David committed not only adultery but also murder and just about every other sin. Yet how did the "Old Testament tyrant," full of vengeance and wrath, react when David confessed his sins? Said Nathan the prophet: "The LORD has forgiven you" (2 Samuel 12:13).

rebellion and sin. Yet he does not leave the guilty unpunished" (Exodus 34:6, 7).

"Therefore consider the **goodness and severity** of God: on those who fell, severity; but **toward you, goodness**, if you continue in His goodness. Otherwise you also will be cut off." (Romans 11:22).

Does God enjoy destroying those who reject His free gift of Salvation?
"Say to them: 'As I live,' says the Lord GOD, 'I have **no pleasure** in the **death** of the **wicked**, but that the wicked turn from his way and live. Turn, turn from your evil ways! For why should you die, O house of Israel?'" (Ezekiel 33:11).

In Isaiah God's people are considered His vineyard. What does He say about His vineyard when it comes time to destroy the wicked?
"And now, O inhabitants of Jerusalem and men of Judah, **judge**, please, between Me and My vineyard. **What more could have been done** to My vineyard **that I have not done** in it? Why then, when I expected it to bring forth good grapes, did it bring forth wild grapes? (Isaiah 5:3, 4).

Why does God do all that He can do to save us?
"The LORD has appeared of old to me, saying: 'Yes, **I have loved you** with an **everlasting love**; Therefore with lovingkindness I have drawn you" (Jeremiah 31:3) .

Or in another place, God the Father says: "'Return, O backsliding children,' says the LORD; 'for I am married to you. I will take you, one from a city and two from a family, and I will bring you to Zion'" (Jeremiah 3:14).

Some tyrant, huh?

Jesus and the Father

A group of ants were about to cross a busy road where they would surely be killed. An ants'-rights activist, wanting to save them, stood above them, shouting, "Don't cross the road!" It wasn't working. Instead, what would have been better would have been for that activist to have become an ant and, as one of them, lead them to safety.

In a real sense, that's what God the Father did for us. Jesus, One with the Father, came down from heaven to humanity to, among other things, show the world what God the Father was really like. As Jesus said: "He who has seen Me has seen the Father" (John 14:9).

You want answers about the nature of God the Father? You want to know what your true Father, your Father in heaven, is like? Look at Jesus, at His kindness, His forgiveness, His love, and, most importantly, His self-sacrifice for the good of others. Remember this picture of Jesus as you understand His statement: "He who has seen Me has seen the Father".

Yes, regardless of the human father earthly fate handed you—a kind and caring man, or the one little Stevie had—you still have another Father who loves you and will, through Jesus, forgive you, no matter your past or how hard you find it to forgive yourself.

WATCH visit **answrs.co/explain** to watch a video answering questions including *What is God's real name?* and *Why does the God of the Old Testament seem a lot less loving than the God of the New Testament?*

JESUS

04

The Question

Interest and controversy had begun to rise about Jesus of Nazareth (Hebrew: *Yeshua Ha-Notzrim*), a Jewish itinerant preacher from the house of David. In the midst of His ministry, Jesus Himself asked His disciples a question with an answer that has changed history.

"Who," Jesus asked, "do men say that I am?" (Mark 8:27).

From the time of Jesus, almost 2000 years ago, to this moment, this question remains perhaps the most divisive question ever asked. People have given up their lives based on their answer to that question; others have taken lives based on their answer to that same question. Some of the greatest acts of selflessness and kindness and some of the most heinous acts of evil—all have been done based on someone's answer to that question. From the time when humans thought the Earth stood immobile in the center of the universe and all heavenly bodies orbited it, until today, when we have peered into the guts of the cosmos—this same question still creates controversy.

Ultimately, only one of two logical answers to this question exists. In this chapter, let's explore those answers for ourselves.

A Poached Egg?

Agnostic-turned-Christian writer C.S. Lewis, framed the issue in a famous quote:

"I am trying here to prevent anyone saying the really foolish thing that people often say about Him: I'm ready to accept Jesus as a great moral teacher, but I don't accept his claim to be God. That is the one thing we must not say. A man who was merely a man and said the sort of things Jesus said would not be a great moral teacher. He would either be a lunatic—on the level with the man who says he is a poached egg—or else he would be the Devil of Hell. You must make your choice. Either this man was, and is, the Son of God, or else a madman or something worse. You can shut him up for a fool, you can spit at him and kill him as a demon or you can fall at his feet and call him Lord and God, but let us not come with any patronizing nonsense about his being a great human teacher. He has not left that open to us. He did not intend to."

Lewis makes a powerful point—the accounts we have of Jesus, that is, of the things Jesus said about Himself, don't leave us with any logical option other than those Lewis expressed here: either Jesus was "a madman or something worse," or He was the divine Son of God.

Why? What did Jesus say that leaves us, logically at least, with only one of those two options?

A Madman in Manhattan

Years ago, a man stood on a street corner in Manhattan and began preaching. You may have seen people like this, a loudspeaker in one hand, a Bible in the other, proclaiming biblical doctrine, usually telling sinners to repent or face judgment and divine wrath, or warning that the end of the world was near.

Suppose, however, that street preacher wasn't telling people about God but, rather, making

WATCH visit **answrs.co/divine** to watch a video answering questions including *Is Jesus fully divine?*, *Did Jesus ever laugh?* and *Who is Michael the Archangel?*

claims about himself which meant that he was, actually, God Himself. What would you think? Most likely, you'd think him a madman.

Well, Jesus of Nazareth, *Yeshua HaNotzrim*, made similar claims about Himself. In His time here on earth, He said things that most everyone who heard understood as meaning that He, indeed, was divine.

Jesus Claims...

For instance, speaking to devoted followers who were mourning the death of a loved one, Jesus said: "I am the resurrection and the life. He who believes in Me, though he may die, he shall live" (John 11:25). The Jews of that time understood, and rightly so, that life came only from God, and that only God could restore life. Thus, Christ's words clearly point to Himself as divine, as God. They could mean nothing else.

When talking with the religious leaders, Jesus said: "Most assuredly, I say to you, before Abraham was, I AM" (John 8:58). His use of the phrase, "I AM," was a direct reference to the book of Exodus, when God referred to Himself as "I AM" (Exodus 3:14). Immediately after Jesus made that statement, the religious leaders "took up stones to throw at Him" (John 8:59), which shows that they understood Jesus to claim to be God. In fact, there was another time when Jesus said something that could be understood as referring to His own divinity, and the religious leaders wanted to stone Him here, too. When Jesus asked why, they responded, "For a good

WATCH

visit **answrs.co/jesus** watch a short video about Jesus. | 2:32

work we do not stone You, but for blasphemy, and because You, being a Man, make Yourself God" (John 10:33).

Speaking to His followers, Jesus said, "I am the way, the truth, and the life" (John 14:6). He didn't say that *He knew* the way, or that *He pointed* to the truth, or that *He could lead* them to life. No—read the words themselves. He said, "I *am* the way, the truth, and the life." Either He was these things—or He was crazy.

When a man in great suffering, a paralytic, was brought before Him, Jesus said: "Son, your sins are

FACT ABOUT JESUS

The odds of 1 person fulfilling 8 prophecies would be 1 in a hundred quadrillion (1:100,000,000,000,000,000). In Jesus' lifetime, he fulfilled not only eight, but more than 150 prophecies!

Q&A FROM THE BIBLE

Who is Jesus?
"The beginning of the gospel of Jesus Christ, the **Son of God**" (Mark 1:1).

Who created everything?
"He has delivered us from the power of darkness and conveyed us into the kingdom of the Son of His love, in whom we have redemption through His blood, the forgiveness of sins. He is the image of the invisible God, the firstborn over all creation. For **by Him all things were created that are in heaven and that are on earth, visible and invisible**, whether thrones or dominions or principalities or powers. **All things** were created **through Him** and for Him. And He is before all things, and in Him all things consist" (Colossians 1:13-17).

Since the Son, Jesus, is the individual who created everything then who is Jesus?
"In the beginning was the Word, and the Word was **with** God, and the Word **was** God. He was in the beginning with God. **All things** were made **through Him**, and without Him nothing was made that was made" (John 1:1-3).

"The virgin shall be with child, and bear a **Son**, and they shall call His name Immanuel," which is translated, '**God with us**." (Matthew 1:23).

Why did God's Son come to Earth as a man?
"And she will bring forth a Son, and you shall call His name Jesus, for He will **save** His people **from their sins**" (Matthew 1:21).

Why does God want to save us?
"For the **wages** of sin is **death**, but the gift of God is eternal life in Christ Jesus our Lord" (Romans 6:26).

Since the penalty for sin is death, what did Jesus do for us?
"For when we were still without strength, in due time **Christ died for the ungodly**" (Romans 5:6).

"But He was wounded for **our transgressions**, He was bruised for **our iniquities**; the chastisement for our peace was upon Him, and by His stripes we are healed" (Isaiah 53:5).

"Who Himself bore **our sins** in His **own body** on the tree, that we, having died to sins, might live for righteousness—by whose stripes you were healed" (1 Peter 2:24).

Since Jesus died for our sins, what do we become when we believe this and accept Jesus as our Lord and Savior?
"For He made Him who knew no sin to be sin for us, that we might become the righteousness of God in Him" (2 Corinthians 5:21).

Did Jesus stay dead after He died?
"Then they went in and **did not find** the body of the Lord Jesus. And it happened, as they were greatly perplexed about this, that behold, two men stood by them in shining garments. Then, as they were afraid and bowed their faces to the earth, they said to them, 'Why do you seek the living among the dead? He is not here, **but is risen**! Remember how He spoke to you when He was still in Galilee, saying, "The Son of Man must be delivered into the hands of sinful men, and be crucified, and the **third day rise again**"'" (Luke 24:3-7).

Where is Jesus today?
"Looking unto Jesus, the author and finisher of our faith, who for the joy that was set before Him endured the cross, despising the shame, and has **sat down** at the right hand of the **throne of God**" (Hebrews 12:2).

Will we ever see Him again?
"In My Father's house are many mansions; if it were not so, I would have told you. I go to **prepare a place for you**. And if I go and prepare a place for you, I will **come again** and receive you to Myself; that **where I am**, there **you may be also**" (John 14:2,3).

LISTEN IN

visit **answrs.co/son** to listen to a presentation that goes along with this chapter.

WATCH

visit **answrs.co/savior** watch a video about our Savior, Jesus Christ

forgiven you" (Mark 2:5), to which the nearby scribes, indignant, responded: "Why does this Man speak blasphemies like this? Who can forgive sins but God alone?" (Mark 2:7). They were right—only God can forgive sins, which, again, is why either Jesus was who He said He was, or He was no different than the madman on the street corner in Manhattan.

Another time, the Bible records this about Jesus in a dispute over how to keep the Sabbath: "Therefore the Jews sought all the more to kill Him, because He not only broke the Sabbath, but also said that God was His Father, making Himself equal with God" (John 5:18). No question, the people who heard Jesus speak understood, very clearly, Jesus' claims to divinity.

Actions

In short, Jesus said numerous things that make no sense unless 1) He was God or 2) He was a liar or a lunatic. The idea of Jesus, having said the things that He said, and yet still being a great moral teacher, is beyond silly.

Yes, Jesus made amazing, even outrageous, claims about Himself. However, unlike anyone else making such claims—Jesus backed up those claims by His actions. That is, Jesus did things that, indeed, proved the divinity He claimed for Himself.

When He said, "I am the resurrection and the life" (John 11:25), what did He do right after? He stood before the tomb of Lazarus, who had been dead four days, and whose body was already decomposing, and said, "'Lazarus, come forth!' And he who had died came out bound hand and foot with graveclothes, and his face was wrapped with a cloth. Jesus said to them, 'Loose him, and let him go.' Then many of the Jews who had come to Mary, and had seen the things Jesus did, believed in Him" (John 11:43-45).

Not only did He forgive the sins of the man in great suffering, He spoke a few words and the man, completely paralyzed, was instantly healed—all to the astonishment of the witnesses (Mark 2:1-11).

Over and over, Jesus backed up His claims to divinity by doing deeds that only a divine being could do, which is why, all through history, millions have believed in the divinity of Jesus. They have good reason to.

"Who Do Men Say That I Am?"

When Jesus had asked the question at the start of this chapter, one of His disciples answered, "You are the Christ, the Son of the living God" (Matthew 16:16), to which Jesus responded, "Blessed are you, Simon Bar-Jonah, for flesh and blood has not revealed this to you, but My Father who is in heaven" (Matthew 16:17).

Though asked thousands of years ago, the question still hovers in the air, even now. Given the things Jesus claimed about Himself—and His deeds that backed up those claims—how each one of us chooses to answer that question remains, no doubt, the most important choice that we, as human flesh and blood, can ever make.

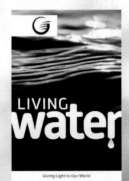

LIVING
water

Giving Light to Our World

05

THE HOLY SPIRIT

Newton's Apple

Most school children have heard the story about Isaac Newton sitting under the apple tree. An apple falls on his head and, *Voila*! Newton discovered gravity. Though the story of the apple falling on his head is, indeed, true, that's not what made him "discover" gravity. (Gravity had already been there before Newton, and others besides Newton knew it, too.)

Instead, after that incident, Newton began to understand an important principle about gravity, which was that it was everywhere. The same force that dropped the apple on his head was the same force, gravity, that kept the moon in orbit around the Earth, the Earth in orbit around the sun, and so forth.

In a loose sense, this image can serve as an analogy for the presence of God in our world through the person of the Holy Spirit. The Holy Spirit? Most everyone has heard of Him, but so often His identity and role remain mysterious.

Who is the Holy Spirit, what does He do, and why is an understanding of His role so important for the Christian today?

Let this, *The Answer Book*, answer these questions.

The Presence

Right before Jesus returned to heaven, after His death and resurrection, He spoke to His followers. Telling them to preach the gospel everywhere, Jesus then said: "Lo, I am with you always, even unto the end of the age" (Matthew 28:20).

What a wonderful promise! But how can that be? Jesus, who took upon Himself a human body, and who still retains that body in heaven—how could He be with His followers even to the end of the world?

The answer is that the Holy Spirit, Himself divine, manifests Himself here instead. He is the

Q&A FROM THE BIBLE

Who is the Holy Spirit?
"But Peter said, 'Ananias, why has Satan filled your heart **to lie** to the **Holy Spirit** and keep back part of the price of the land for yourself? While it remained, was it not your own? And after it was sold, was it not in your own control? Why have you conceived this thing in your heart? You have **not lied** to men **but to God**" (Acts 5:3, 4).

Does the Holy Spirit think?
"For it **seemed good to the Holy Spirit**, and to us, to lay upon you no greater burden than these necessary things" (Acts 15:28)

Does the Holy Spirit teach?
"For the Holy Spirit will **teach you** in that very hour what you ought to say" (Luke 12:12).

Does the Holy Spirit speak?
"While Peter thought about the vision, the **Spirit said to him**, "Behold, three men are seeking you" (Acts 10:19).

Since we see that the Holy Spirit is a member of the Godhead and interacts with us what is His specific role?

representative, the very presence of God now on Earth.

His Divinity

As we saw in the previous chapter, Jesus Himself was God; it's the same with the Holy Spirit. Christians don't believe in three Gods but one God who exists in three persons. As respected author and theologian Wayne Grudem wrote: "God eternally exists as three persons, Father, Son, and Holy Spirit, and each person is fully God, and there is one God" (*Systematic Theology*, Zondervan, 1994, p. 226). The Father is God, the Son is God, and the Holy Spirit is God.

For example, in what name did Jesus say that people were to be baptized? "Go therefore and make disciples of all nations, baptizing them in the name of the Father and of the Son and of the Holy Spirit" (Matthew 28:19). The Father is God, the Son is God, and, indeed, the sentence makes sense only if the Holy Spirit is God as well. That formula alone puts the Holy Spirit on par with the Father and the Son.

His Personhood

Because the Holy Spirit is sometimes depicted in the Bible with images such as fire or wind, some argue that He is an impersonal power,

Pastor John Bradshaw

WATCH

visit **answrs.co/spirit** to watch a short video about the Holy Spirit | 2:23

kind of like an electric current. However, too many texts refer to Him in ways that make sense only if He, like the Father and Son, is a person:

"However, when He, the Spirit of truth, has come, He will guide you into all truth; for He will not speak on His own authority, but whatever He hears He will speak; and He will tell you things to come" (John 16:13).

"Now He who searches the hearts knows what the mind of the Spirit is, because He makes intercession for the saints according to the will of God" (Romans 8:27).

"But the Helper, the Holy Spirit, whom the Father will send in My name, He will teach you all things, and bring to your remembrance all

"But the Helper, the Holy Spirit, whom the Father will send in My name, He will teach you all things, and **bring to your remembrance** all things that I said to you" (John 14:26).

"Nevertheless I tell you the truth. It is to your advantage that I go away; for if I do not go away, the Helper will not come to you; but if I depart, I will send Him to you. And when He has come, He will **convict** the world **of sin**, and **of righteousness**, and **of judgment**" (John 16:7,8).

"However, when He, the Spirit of truth, has come, He will **guide you into all truth**" (John 16:13).

"That He would grant you, according to the riches of His glory, to be **strengthened with might through His Spirit** in the inner man" (Ephesians 3:16).

How do we receive the help of the Holy Spirit?
"If a son asks for bread from any father among you, will he give him a stone? Or if he asks for a fish, will he give him a serpent instead of a fish? Or if he asks for an egg, will he offer him a scorpion? If you then, being evil, know how to give good gifts to your children, how much more will your heavenly Father **give the Holy Spirit to those who ask** Him!" (Luke 11:11-13).

things that I said to you" (John 14:26).

"But God has revealed them to us through His Spirit. For the Spirit searches all things, yes, the deep things of God" (1 Corinthians 2:10).

"Now I beg you, brethren, through the Lord Jesus Christ, and through the love of the Spirit, that you strive together with me in prayers to God for me" (Romans 15:30).

The Holy Spirit, guides, teaches, intercedes for us, speaks, searches the heart, and searches the deep things of God. A cold, impersonal force doing all these things? Not likely. Also, Paul talked about the "love of the Spirit." An impersonal force who loves? No. Only a personal being can show love. These texts make sense only if the Holy Spirit is a person, not some impersonal force, such as electricity.

Gravity and Grace

Of all that the Holy Spirit does, the apostle Paul expressed His most important role: "No one can say that Jesus is Lord except by the Holy Spirit" (1 Corinthians 12:3). In other words, the Holy Spirit's job is to make us realize our need of the

WATCH

visit **answrs.co/work** to watch the video
The Work of the Spirit | 58:31

Q&A: The Holy Spirit

WATCH visit **answrs.co/force** to

watch a video answering questions including *Is the Holy Spirit a person or a force?*, *How do you know that the Holy Spirit is God?* and *Why did Jesus say that the Holy Spirit couldn't come unless He left?*

salvation that we are offered, freely, by God's grace in Jesus Christ.

Just as gravity pulls on all matter, the Holy Spirit pulls on all human hearts. Most people, even the most corrupt, have some sense of morality, of right and wrong. If we were just a complicated mix of sub-atomic particles, and nothing more—then it would be hard to explain our sense of good and evil. Atoms, even lots of them stuck together, don't know good from evil.

If, however, we are beings created in the image of God, and the Holy Spirit is the presence of God here on earth now, then morality, the sense of right and wrong, becomes much easier to understand—especially when Jesus Himself said that the Holy Spirit will "convict the world of sin, and of righteousness, and of judgment" (John 16:8).

Feeling, perhaps, convicted of sin (that you have done it), or of righteousness (that you are lacking it), or of a judgment (that if there were one you might not fare so well in it)? These thoughts, and the mere fact that you are reading *The Answer Book*, shows that the Holy Spirit is pulling you toward God just as surely as gravity pulled Newton's apple to the earth.

LISTEN IN

visit **answrs.co/comforter** to listen to a presentation that goes along with this chapter.

06

SALVATION

In 1895, William Roentgen discovered invisible rays that could penetrate material objects that human eyes couldn't. Though taken for granted today, X-rays were quite the hoot back then—the kind of thing more likely found in a circus than in a medical institution.

However, X-rays soon made their way into every hospital. Early on, someone had a full body X-ray at a sanitarium in Switzerland. When he saw the photo, that of his entire skeleton, he exclaimed: "I have just seen what I will look like dead!"

The Book of Dead Philosophers

Macabre, yes, but the patient had a point. We will all one day be only our skeleton, if that. No matter who we are, what we accomplish, how famous we become, how many orphans we adopt, how many skyscrapers we build, how many armies we command, or how many hungry mouths we feed—you will die, everyone you ever helped will die, and every memory of you and everything that you have ever done or said will vanish into oblivion.

At least that's one option, anyway.

As the author *The Book of Dead Philosophers* expressed it: "This book begins from the simple assumption: what defines human life on our corner of the planet at the present time is not just a fear of death, but an overwhelming terror of annihilation. This is a terror both of the inevitability of our demise with its future prospect of pain and possibly meaningless suffering, and the horror of what lies in the grave other than our body nailed in a box and lowered into the earth to become wormwood."

Maybe the author's overstating the case; maybe not. Either way, what does the future hold for us if not, ultimately, death?

And, thus, the question is: What does our death, and the inevitability of our death, do to the meaning of our life? That is, what can lives that are lived here, but forgotten forever once they're gone, finally mean?

The Myth of Sisyphus

One of the most famous writers of the twentieth century was Frenchman Albert Camus. An atheist, Camus struggled with the questions posed above. How do you live a life that, he believed, was meaningless? Is life worth living, given all the pain and suffering, since it always ends in death, anyway?

One of his books, *The Myth of Sisyphus*, was based on the ancient myth about a man condemned by the gods to eternal punishment. Sisyphus had to push a boulder up a hill, only to have it roll down, repeating this over and over again ... the idea being that there was no greater punishment than fruitless toil.

For Camus, the plight of Sisyphus was a good metaphor for human existence and the apparent fruitlessness of it. He began the book with this, perhaps the most controversial line in

WATCH visit **answrs.co/ salvation** to watch a short video about God's free gift | 3:06

Q&A FROM THE BIBLE

How many of us have sinned?
"For **all** have sinned and fall short of the glory of God" (Romans 3:23).

What does my sin, or iniquity, do to my connection with God?
"But your **iniquities** have **separated** you from your God; and your sins have hidden His face from you" (Isaiah 59:2).

What is God's desire in regard to us?
"And let them make Me a sanctuary, that I may **dwell among them**" (Exodus 25:8).

"Behold, the virgin shall be with child, and bear a Son, and they shall call His name Immanuel, which is translated, '**God with us**'" (Matthew 1:23).

What is the consequence, or result, of our sin?
"For the wages of sin is death" (Romans 6:23).

What did God give so that we wouldn't have to experience this eternal death?
"For God so loved the world that He gave His only begotten Son, that whoever believes in Him should not perish but have everlasting life" (John 3:16).

"For the wages of sin is death, but the gift of God is eternal life in Christ Jesus our Lord" (Romans 6:23).

What was the motive of Jesus, the Son of God, in coming to our world?
"This is a faithful saying and worthy of all acceptance, that Christ Jesus came into the world **to save sinners**, of whom I am chief" (1 Timothy 1:15).

"And she will bring forth a Son, and you shall call His name Jesus, for He will **save** His people **from their sins**" (Matthew 1:21).

What exactly did Jesus do for me that I might experience being saved from my sins?
But He was **wounded for our transgressions**, He was **bruised for our iniquities**; The chastisement for our peace was upon Him, and by His stripes we are healed" (Isaiah 53:5).

"And you know that He was manifested to **take away our sins**, and in Him there is no sin" (1 John 3:5).

"Christ also suffered for us. … who Himself **bore** our sins **in His own body** on the tree, that we, having died to sins, might live for righteousness—by whose stripes you were healed" (1 Peter 2:21, 24).

Who can come to God to receive this gift?
"And the Spirit and the bride say, "**Come**!" And let him who hears say, "**Come**!" And let him who thirsts come. **Whoever desires**, let him **take** the water of life **freely**" (Revelation 22:17).

"All that the Father gives Me will come to Me, and the one who comes to Me I will by **no means cast out**" (John 6:37).

How do I give my sins over to Jesus and experience forgiveness and freedom from sin?
"If we **confess our sins**, He is faithful and just to **forgive us** our sins and to cleanse us from all unrighteousness" (1 John 1:9).

After God takes my sin and forgives me do I still need to be trapped in repeating it?
"Knowing this, that our old man was crucified with Him, that the body of sin might be done away with, that we should **no longer be slaves of sin** … Therefore do not let sin reign in your mortal body, that you should obey it in its lusts … For **sin shall not have dominion over you**,

WATCH visit answrs.co/saved to

watch a video answering *How can I know that I am saved?* and more

twentieth century literature: "There is but one truly serious philosophical problem, and that is suicide. Judging whether life is or is not worth living amounts to answering the fundamental question of philosophy."

Kind of a bummer, eh? Camus wasn't advocating suicide. He was just expressing the difficult question: Is a life without meaning worth living?

Rotten Souls

Compare, though, Camus' words with these found in the Bible: "For I am persuaded that neither death nor life, nor angels nor principalities nor powers, nor things present nor things to come, nor height nor depth, nor any other created thing, shall be able to separate us from the love of God which is in Christ Jesus our Lord" (Romans 8:38, 39).

What a contrast! And that's because Paul believed in Jesus and the promise of eternal life found in Jesus. That is, Paul had salvation—and, in this, he found the meaning of life.

It's simple. We are sinners. We have all done wrong. You don't think so? Ask yourself this question: *Suppose you had to stand before an all-knowing, all-powerful, and holy God who knew everything about you, everything. From your darkest thoughts to the secret deeds that you'd rather be dead than let others know about.*

How would you do before Him who, indeed, knew everything, even all that you have tried to forget? If that thought scares you,

it ought to, because the Bible makes it clear that we are, all of us, rotten souls. In Romans chapter 3, Paul talks about humanity, saying that none are righteous, our throats are tombs, our lips are filled with poison, our feet are swift to shed blood and on and on ... and that's only the half of it.

But Paul also writes this: "But God demonstrates His own love toward us, in that while we were still sinners, Christ died for us." (Romans 5:8). *While we were yet sinners* ... that is, despite all the nasty, hateful, and seemingly unforgiveable things that you have done (things that you can't seem to forgive yourself for, anyway)—Christ died for you, not despite these things but because of them.

That same God, whom you'd be afraid to stand before because of all your foul deeds—that same God, in the person of Jesus, bore all those foul deeds upon Himself at the cross. The punishment that you deserve for those deeds fell, instead, on Jesus Christ so that you—however undeserving—don't have to face the punishment for those same deeds yourself.

This is the gospel, this is the plan of salvation: total forgiveness freely offered you, regardless of your past. You can't earn it; you can't make yourself good enough to deserve it. Instead, it's yours, by faith. You need to repent, admit your sins, and ask Jesus into your life, and, instantly, by faith, you can have the assurance that when you do stand before God in judgment, you have already been accepted by Him. Not for your sake (despite it, actually) but because of Jesus and His sacrifice for you.

No wonder it is called "the Good News."

LISTEN IN visit answrs.co/gift to listen to a presentation that goes along with what you're reading in this chapter.

WATCH visit **answrs.co/hope** to watch

the video *Is there hope for a planet in crisis?*

58:30

Ready for Baptism

Years ago, an American pastor, Howard Mumma, was preaching in an American church in Paris. He had a visitor who, eventually, studied the Bible with the pastor, but in secret. No one could know. The visitor had told him, "The reason I have been coming to church is because I am seeking. I'm almost on a pilgrimage—seeking something to fill the void that I am experiencing—and no one else knows."

One day, his student asked him about baptism.

"Howard," he asked, "do you perform baptisms?"

When he said that he did, the student asked, "What is the significance of this rite?" After the pastor explained, much to his thrilled amazement, the man said, "Howard, I am ready. I want this. This is what I want to commit my life to."

The man? At that time, the world's most well-known atheist: Albert Camus.

Unfortunately, before he could be baptized, Camus died. Had he, a sinner, given his heart to Jesus, Camus would have known the reality of what God offers us all—the gift of salvation.

READ MORE + SHARE THIS TOPIC

Visit **www.glowonline.org/answer/gift** to read more about what you just read here. You can also share it on social media.

for you are not under law but under grace" (Romans 6:6, 12, 14).

"Therefore, if anyone is **in Christ**, he is a **new creation**; old things have passed away; behold, all things have become new" (2 Corinthians 5:17).

What is this experience called of becoming a new creature and receiving the gift of eternal life?
"Jesus answered and said to him, 'Most assuredly, I say to you, unless one is **born again**, he cannot see the kingdom of God'" (John 3:3).

How can I daily be born again?
"Having been **born again**, not of corruptible seed but incorruptible, **through the word of God** which lives and abides forever" (1 Peter 1:23).

What did Jesus say God's word shows us?
"You search the **Scriptures**, for in them you think you have eternal life; and these are they which **testify of Me**" (John 5:39).

Why is it important that we spend time every day connecting with Jesus through the Bible?
"Jesus said to him, "I am the way, the truth, and the life. No one comes to the Father except through Me" (John 14:6).

"Nor is there salvation in any other, for there is no other name under heaven given among men by which we must be saved" (Acts 4:10,12).

Jesus Christ, the faithful witness, the firstborn from the dead, and the ruler over the kings of the earth. To Him who *Loved* us and washed us from our sins in His own blood

Revelation 1:5

07

BAPTISM

Death, Then Life

In the last chapter, we read about one of the most famous atheists in the twentieth century, Frenchman Albert Camus, requesting baptism. Camus had been impacted by the Holy Spirit (see chapter 5, "Newton's Apple"), prompting him to make this decision.

Albert Camus wanting baptism? That would be, today, like the head of ISIS wanting to convert to Judaism. Most people know about the Christian practice of baptism and that Christians deem it important. What, then, is the meaning and purpose of this practice? What does it represent, and why should anyone who, like Camus, wants to follow Jesus seek to be baptized?

Hope You Drown!

A young 23-year-old man had his eyes opened after studying the Bible. He came face-to-face with the fact that, sure—though he was no rapist, serial killer, drug dealer, or the like—he was still a sinner in need of salvation. Having been convicted of his sins and repenting of them, he openly professed belief in Jesus as his Savior and asked Jesus to cover his sins with His shed blood and perfect righteousness.

This is what is known as "salvation by faith." The young man knew that nothing he could do could earn what Christ offered him. It was, instead, a gift, given solely by grace, which is undeserved favor. In short, he accepted the great news that, by faith in Jesus, he could receive the promise of eternal life, no matter how unworthy he felt and, in fact, was.

Then, after making the decision to be baptized, he told his sister, who responded negatively.

"I hope you drown!" she said.

Her remark was cruel, yet fascinatingly enough, there's a great deal of truth in it. That's because, in a way, baptism does signify death—the death of the old person, a sinner alienated from God, who then becomes a new person in Jesus Christ.

If You Believe...

All through the New Testament, we find the early church not only teaching about baptism but, repeatedly performing it. For instance, right after Saul of Tarsus, the great persecutor of the early church, become a follower of Jesus—what happened? He was temporarily blinded (see Acts 9:8,9). The Bible says that, after he had been prayed for to regain his sight—then "immediately there fell from his eyes something like scales: and he received his sight at once, and arose, and was baptized" (Acts 9:18).

Another time, when Philip had witnessed to an

WATCH

visit **answrs.co/baptism** to watch a short video about baptism and what it means for us | 2:54

WATCH

visit **answrs.co/ready** to watch a video answering questions including *Is baptism essential for salvation?*, *Does a person have to be re-baptized?* and *When is a person ready to be baptized, and what are the qualifications?*

official from a foreign court who had accepted Jesus, the man immediately requested to be baptized: "Then Philip said, 'If you believe with all your heart, you may.' And he answered and said, 'I believe that Jesus Christ is the Son of God.' So he commanded the chariot to stand still. And both Philip and the eunuch went down into the water, and he baptized him" (Acts 8:37-38).

Dead, Then Alive

What, then, does this mean, this rite of baptism? In the book of Romans, the apostle Paul explains: "Or do you not know that as many of us as were baptized into Christ Jesus were baptized into His death? Therefore, we were buried with Him through baptism into death, that just as Christ was raised from the dead by the glory of the Father, even so we also should walk in newness of life" (Romans 6:3, 4).

The idea is simply this: When we accept Jesus Christ, we have a new life in Him, a whole new start, a whole new beginning. Jesus Himself had said, "You must be born again" (John 3:7). Baptism by immersion (the Greek word for "baptize" means "to immerse"), that is, when you

What was the last command of Jesus in the book of Matthew?
"Go therefore and **make disciples** of all the nations, **baptizing** them in the name of the Father and of the Son and of the Holy Spirit, **teaching them** to observe all things that I have commanded you; and lo, I am with you always, even to the end of the age." Amen (Matthew 28:18-20).

What did Peter tell the people after preaching?
"Now when they heard this, they were cut to the heart, and said to Peter and the rest of the apostles, 'Men and brethren, what shall we do?' Then Peter said to them, 'Repent, and let **every one** of you **be baptized** in the name of Jesus Christ for the remission of sins; and you shall receive the **gift of the Holy Spirit**'" (Acts 2:37,38).

Is Baptism necessary?
"Jesus answered, 'Most assuredly, I say to you, unless one is born of **water** and the **Spirit**, he cannot enter the kingdom of God.'" (John 3:5)

"He who believes **and is baptized** will be saved; but he who does not believe will be condemned" (Mark 16:16).

What does baptism represent?
"…do you not know that as many of us as were **baptized into Christ** Jesus were **baptized into His death**? Therefore we were **buried** with Him **through baptism** into death, that just as Christ was raised from the dead by the glory of the Father, even so we also should walk in newness of life" (Romans 6:3,4).

What are pre-requisites to being baptized?
"Then Philip opened his mouth, and beginning

at this Scripture, preached Jesus to him. Now as they went down the road, they came to some water. And the eunuch said, 'See, here is water. What hinders me from being baptized?' Then Philip said, '**If you believe** with all your heart, you may.' And he answered and said, '**I believe** that **Jesus Christ is the Son of God**.' So he commanded the chariot to stand still. And both Philip and the eunuch went down into the water, and he baptized him (Acts 8:35-38).

"Peter said to them, '**Repent**, and let every one of you be baptized in the name of Jesus Christ for the remission of sins; and you shall receive the gift of the Holy Spirit'" (Acts 2:38).

"Jesus said to His disciples, 'If anyone desires to come after Me, let him **deny himself**, and **take up his cross**, and **follow Me**'" (Matthew 16:24).

What does the believer receive when they are baptized?

"Then Peter said to them, 'Repent, and let every one of you be baptized in the name of Jesus Christ for the remission of sins; and you shall receive the **gift of the Holy Spirit**" (Acts 2:38).

What do we join when we are baptized?

"Then those who gladly received his word **were baptized**; and that day about three thousand souls were **added to them**" (Acts 2:48).

"For as the body is one and has many members, but all the members of that one body, being many, are one body, so also is Christ. For by one Spirit we were **all baptized into one body**—whether Jews or Greeks, whether slaves or free—and have all been made to drink into one Spirit. For in fact the body is not one member but many… Now you are the **body of Christ**, and members individually" (1 Corinthians 12:12-14, 27).

What do we "put on" when we are baptized?

"For as many of you as were baptized into Christ have **put on Christ**" (Galatians 3:27).

What does it look like when we put off the old man and put on Christ?

" Do not lie to one another, since you have **put off the old man** with his deeds, and have **put on the new man** who is renewed in knowledge according to the image of Him who created him… Therefore, as the elect of God, holy and beloved, **put on** tender mercies, kindness, humility, meekness, longsuffering; bearing with one another, and forgiving one another, if anyone has a complaint against another; even as Christ forgave you, so you also must do. But above all these things put on love, which is the bond of perfection" (Colossians 1:9-14).

"Therefore, if anyone is **in Christ**, he is a **new creation**; old things have passed away; behold, all things have become new" (2 Corinthians 5:17).

What should we do now?

"And now why are you waiting? **Arise and be baptized**, and wash away your sins, calling on the name of the Lord" (Acts 22:16).

What happens after baptism?

"If then you were raised with Christ, **seek those things which are above**, where Christ is, sitting at the right hand of God. **Set your mind on things above**, not on things on the earth. For you died, and your life is hidden with Christ in God" (Colossians 3:1-3).

"As you therefore have received Christ Jesus the Lord, so walk in Him, rooted and built up in Him and established in the faith, as you have been taught, abounding in it with thanksgiving" (Colossians 2:6, 7).

From Greek baptizo: *to immerse, dip under*

WATCH

visit **answrs.co/forgotten** to watch the video *Buried and Forgotten by God.*

58:31

go fully under the water, symbolizing the death to your old person, the person who lived a sinful life apart from God. But when you accept Jesus, that old person dies. (Hence, why the young man's sister's cutting remarks were closer to the truth than she realized.)

When immersed, of course, you don't stay under the water. You come up, a symbol of your new life in Jesus, in which you have repented of your sins, put them away, and live as a new person in Christ. "For as many of you as have been baptized into Christ have put on Christ" (Galatians 3:27). Your old ways of living, your old habits, your old patterns (at least the sinful ones), are now, in a sense, washed away, and you now have a new beginning, a new life, in Jesus Christ.

An Open Profession

In essence, by getting baptized, we openly profess our faith in the death and resurrection of Jesus Christ and that we now, by faith, will walk in "the newness of life" offered us by God in Jesus. This doesn't mean we suddenly are perfect, flawless, never again to sin. It means, instead, that we, no doubt impacted by the Holy Spirit, have made a conscious choice to give our lives to Jesus, to obey His commands, and work for the uplifting of His church and of others. By baptism we choose, too, to unite ourselves with a body of like-minded believers, the church, and work together for the edification of the church and of others.

Baptism, however, must be a conscious choice by a person of an accountable age. The old tradition of sprinkling babies is not found in the Bible and, thus, does not count as a *bona fide* baptism. Someone who accepts Jesus as an adult needs more than being sprinkled as an infant. However important, baptism is not a work; it doesn't bestow merit on anyone. It is, instead, a symbol of the new life someone has in Jesus, after accepting the eternal life that Christ has offered.

Thus, though Camus never had a chance to be baptized, his desire to be provides powerful evidence that, yes, he had accepted Jesus. Too bad, however, that by his untimely death in a car accident, he didn't get the chance, by baptism, to publicly declare it.

LISTEN IN visit **answrs.co/reborn** to listen to a presentation that goes along with what you're reading in this chapter.

THE GREAT CONTROVERSY

08

Extra-Terrestrials

Many people remember Steven Spielberg's 1982 Oscar-winning flick, *E.T.*, about a friendly alien, an extraterrestrial who befriends a few kids who help him get home. *E.T.* was quite a different extraterrestrial from the malevolent and evil ones that wreaked havoc here in the 1996 movie *Independence Day*.

Suppose, however, the existence of extraterrestrials wasn't just movie stuff. The universe is, after all, a vast place, extending for billions of light-years. (A light-year is how fast light, moving at 186,000 miles *per second*, can travel in a year). It's filled with two trillion galaxies, each containing billions of stars, many surrounded by planets. No wonder a whole branch of science,

called "astro-biology," seeks out the existence of extraterrestrial life.

However, as these scientists point their powerful devices toward the heavens in hope of retrieving an intelligent peep or mutter from beyond the stars, the Bible not only talks about the existence of extraterrestrial life but has given us some fascinating insights into what this life is like.

What does the Bible say about this extraterrestrial life, and what does it mean for us here today?

E.T.s in the Bible

Here are just a few of the many Bible texts which make it clear that, as far as intelligent life in the universe, we are not alone.

Q&A FROM THE BIBLE

Where was the first war that began all wars?
"And **war** broke out **in heaven**: Michael and his angels fought with the dragon; and the dragon and his angels fought" (Revelation 12:7).

Who is the dragon?
"So the great dragon was cast out, that serpent of old, **called the Devil and Satan**, who deceives the whole world" (Revelation 12:9).

What happened to the dragon and his angels?
"But they did **not prevail**, nor was a place found for them in heaven any longer. So the great dragon was **cast out**, that serpent of old,

called the Devil and Satan, who deceives the whole world; he was **cast to the earth**, and his angels were cast out with him" (Revelation 12:8,9).

Was Satan created defective or evil?
"You were the anointed cherub who covers; I established you; You were on the holy mountain of God; You walked back and forth in the midst of fiery stones. **You were perfect** in your ways from the day you were created, **till iniquity was found** in you" (Ezekiel 28:14, 15).

Since Satan was perfect when he was created what changed to cause him to be found with iniquity, or sin?
"Your **heart was lifted up** because of your beauty; **you corrupted** your wisdom for the sake of your splendor; I cast you to the ground, I laid you before kings, that they might gaze at you." (Ezekiel 28:17).

LISTEN IN

visit **answrs.co/controversy** to listen to a presentation that goes along with this chapter.

"For our wrestling is not against flesh and blood, but against the principalities, against the powers, against the world-rulers of this darkness, against the spiritual hosts of wickedness in the heavenly places" (Ephesians 6:12, ASV).

"His intent was that now, through the church, the manifold wisdom of God should be made known to the rulers and authorities in the heavenly realms" (Ephesians 3:10, NIV).

"For by him all things were created: things in heaven and on earth, visible and invisible, whether thrones or powers or rulers or authorities; all things were created by him and for him" (Colossians 1:16, NIV).

"And there was war in heaven: Michael and his angels fought against the dragon; and the dragon fought and his angels, And prevailed not; neither was their place found any more in heaven. And the great dragon was cast out, that old

WATCH visit **answrs.co/conflict** to watch a short video about the great controversy | 3:01

visit **answrs.co/signs** to watch the video *Seeing the Signs.* | 58:30

serpent, called the Devil, and Satan, which deceiveth the whole world: he was cast out into the earth, and his angels were cast out with him. ... Therefore rejoice, ye heavens, and ye that dwell in them" (Revelation 12:7-12, KJV).

"But though we, or an angel from heaven, preach any other gospel unto you than that which we have preached unto you, let him be accursed" (Galatians 1:8, KJV).

What specifically was Satan thinking that caused him to be corrupted?
"For you have said in your heart: 'I will ascend into heaven, I will **exalt my throne** above the **stars of God**; I will also sit on the mount of the congregation on the farthest sides of the north;I will **ascend above** the heights of the clouds, I will be **like the Most High**'" (Isaiah 14:13-14).

What do the stars of God represent?
"The mystery of the seven stars which you saw in My right hand, and the seven golden lampstands: The **seven stars** are **the angels** of the seven churches" (Revelation 1:20).

Since Satan wanted to be above the other angels and to be like God what did he use to get the other angles to follow him?
"And another sign appeared in heaven: behold, a great, fiery red dragon having seven heads and ten horns, and seven diadems on

his heads. **His tail** drew a **third of the stars** of heaven and threw them to the earth" (Revelation 12:3,4).

What does the tail represent that was Satan's technique to draw a third of the angles to follow him?
"The elder and honorable, he is the head; **the prophet who teaches lies**, he is the tail" (Isaiah 9:15).

When God made man what was the one simple test of love and loyalty that He gave?
"And the LORD God commanded the man, saying, 'Of every tree of the garden you may freely eat; but of the tree of the knowledge of good and evil **you shall not eat**, for in the day that you eat of it you shall surely die'" (Genesis 2:16,17).

"Be sober, be vigilant; because your adversary the devil, as a roaring lion, walketh about, seeking whom he may devour" (1 Peter 5:8, KJV).

Cosmic Conflict

However clear these texts are on the existence of angelic forces, that is, intelligences and powers from another part of the cosmos, not all of them are exactly the friendly character in Spielberg's *E.T.* On the contrary—Scripture tells us that many are evil, hostile to humanity, and have thrown us into the midst of a great cosmic conflict that, though starting in another part of the universe, is being waged here.

People can sense the battle, too, even if they don't know its origins. Friedrich Nietzsche, perhaps the most famous atheist in the nineteenth century, wrote: "Let us conclude. The two oppos-

Q&A FROM THE BIBLE

What did Satan tell Eve would happen if she ate this fruit?
"Then the serpent said to the woman, 'You will **not surely die**. For God knows that in the day you eat of it **your eyes will be opened**, and you will **be like God**, knowing good and evil" (Genesis 3:4).

What did Eve do as a result of her interactions with Satan?
"So when the woman saw that the tree was good for food, that it was pleasant to the eyes, and a tree desirable to make one wise, **she took of its fruit and ate**. She also gave to her husband with her, **and he ate**" (Genesis 3:6).

We saw Satan used lies to deceive both heavenly angels and Adam and Eve. Will he use lies to deceive us today?
"That which has been is what will be, **that which is done** is **what will be done**, and there is **nothing new** under the sun" (Ecclesiastes 1:9).

What did Adam and Eve have over the earth when they were created?
"Then God said, 'Let Us make man in Our image, according to Our likeness; let them have **dominion** over the fish of the sea, over the birds of the air, and over the cattle, over all the earth and over every creeping thing that creeps on the earth'" (Genesis 1:26).

What did Adam and Eve become when they decided to obey Satan?
"Do you not know that to whom you present yourselves **slaves** to obey, you are that one's **slaves whom you obey**, whether of sin leading to death, or of obedience leading to righteousness?" (Romans 1:16).

What did Satan become once man became slaves to sin?
"Now is the judgment of this world; now the **ruler of this world** will be cast out" (John 12:31).

"I will no longer talk much with you, for the **ruler of this world** is coming, and he has nothing in Me" (John 14:30).

"In which you once walked according to the course of this world, according to the **prince of the power of the air**, the spirit who now works in the sons of disobedience" (Ephesians 2:2).

What did God promise would happen?
"And I will put enmity between you and the woman, and between your seed and her Seed; **He shall bruise your head**, and you shall bruise His heel" (Genesis 3:15).

"Inasmuch then as the children have partaken of flesh and blood, He Himself likewise shared in the same, that through death He **might destroy him** who had the power of death, that is, **the devil**, and release those who through fear of death were all their lifetime subject to bondage" (Hebrews 2:14, 15).

Q&A: The Great Controversy

WATCH

visit **answrs.co/destroy** to watch a video answering questions including *Why didn't God just destroy lucifer when he rebelled?* and *How did Lucifer manage to deceive a third of the angels in heaven?*

ing values 'good and bad,' 'good and evil' have been engaged in a fearful struggle on earth for thousands of years."

The American poet T.S. Eliot also wrote:
The world turns and the world changes
But one thing does not change.
In all of my years, one thing does not change;
The perpetual struggle of Good and Evil.

The fact is, through no choice of our own, we exist in a world in which law and lawlessness, good and evil, right and wrong, struggle for supremacy. Every day our thoughts, actions, words place us on one side or another in this great spiritual conflict. However fuzzy at times its manifestations appear—there are only two sides, only two choices: good and evil, truth and error, Christ or Satan. And this battle is being played out at every level of human existence, from the interplay of nations to the quiet struggles in all of us.

Who, at times, hasn't felt this struggle within their own soul?

The Victory at the Cross

How, then, did this great controversy start?

God is the sovereign Creator of all created existence, and the moral foundation of His creation is based on love. And love, to be love, must be freely given. Just as God does not force anyone

to love or follow Him today, He didn't force the angels in heaven to love Him, either. Some of these beings, using the sacred gift of free will that is inherent in love, rebelled—and there was war in heaven, a war that eventually came to earth as well: "Woe to the inhabiters of the earth and of the sea! for the devil is come down unto you, having great wrath, because he knoweth that he hath but a short time" (Revelation 12:12, KJV).

The good news is that 2000 years ago, at the cross, Jesus Christ won the decisive victory in this great controversy. By giving His own life, by sacrificing Himself for us, Christ proved Satan's charges against God wrong, won the planet back to God, and guaranteed the cosmic conflict's ultimate resolution, in which only good triumphs and evil will be forever eradicated.

Because Christ gave His life for us, we can, by faith, share in His victory now, which means that by uniting with Him, we can find power in Him to make the right choices even now in this great controversy. We can be assured that, because of the cross, our death is only a temporary sleep from which we will awake in a new body in a whole new existence.

Those promises are as real as the conflicts we sometimes feel in our own souls here and now, expressions indeed of this great controversy.

WAR IN HEAVEN

READ MORE + SHARE THIS TOPIC

Visit **www.glowonline.org/answer/controversy** to read more about what you just read here. You can also share it on social media.

09

SUFFERING

On Human Suffering

Many consider Fyodor Dostoyevsky the world's greatest novelist and his novel, *The Brothers Karamazov*, the world's greatest novel. Many, too, claim that the chapter, "The Grand Inquisitor," is the greatest in the book. So, what is the theme of what many consider the greatest chapter in the greatest novel written by the world's greatest writer?

If God is all-loving, all-knowing, all-powerful—why is there so much suffering?

That's a tough question; perhaps, the greatest and most important question ever.

What God Cannot Do

Scripture says that "God is love," (1 John 4:8), and love is the foundation of His government. Which means, as we saw in the last chapter, that love, to be love, must be freely given or it is not love at all. To force love is to destroy it. God can force us to fear Him, to obey Him, and to praise Him—but not to love Him.

As we saw, intelligences in another part of the cosmos abused that freedom and rebelled against God, bringing their rebellion to the Earth as well. As human beings, we, too, experience the reality of the freedom inherent in love, too. God does not force us, even now, to follow Him.

A Progression of Questions

However, this important truth leads to a number of questions.

For starters: If, as Scripture teaches, God is all-knowing—"I make known the end from the beginning, from ancient times, what is still to come. I say: My purpose will stand, and I will do all that I please" (Isaiah 46:9, 10, NIV)—then He must have known that some of the angels in heaven, and humans on Earth, would rebel and bring suffering to the world.

This thought leads to another question: Knowing all the evil, pain, and suffering the free will that is inherent in love would bring why did God create us at all?

The answer is that, if God is also all-loving, then we can trust that, somehow, in His love and in His providence and power, He is going to make everything good. He is going to show, in the end, the reality of His love and goodness and fairness and justice, even despite the great controversy and the incredible suffering that it has brought to humanity. We just need to trust in Him now. "Trust in the LORD with all your heart and lean not on your own understanding" (Proverbs 3:5).

This now leads to one more question—the biggest of all.

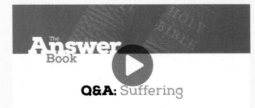

Q&A: Suffering

WATCH

visit **answrs.co/why** to watch a video answering questions including *Why do bad things happen to really good people? What purpose does suffering play in God's plan?* and *How do you know when God will heal?*

WATCH visit **answrs.co/hope** to watch the video *Is there hope for a planet in crisis?*

58:31

How right is it that God is in heaven, being worshipped and praised by unfallen angels, while us poor schnooks, through no choice of our own (that is, none of us ever asked to be born) are caught here on Earth in the midst of this great battle, which began in heaven over challenges to God's love and goodness? That is, whatever the grand issues are about God's love and goodness and justice, which are going to be answered and worked out here amid human suffering, toil, sweat, and blood—how fair is it that while all this happens on Earth, God remains safe and secure up in heaven, far removed from the sometimes-hellish existence here?

Good question. But the answer is even better!

Other People's Pain

Ever hear the common phrase "I feel your pain"? There's one problem, though. However well intentioned, the words are a lie. You never feel anyone's pain except your own. The pain that you might feel over someone else's pain and sorrow is still, always and only, your own pain and your own sorrow, never theirs. You can no more feel another person's pain than you can sweat another person's sweat or shed another person's tears.

You can clutch a quivering and crying person in your arms, with their every quiver pushing up against your flesh and their every cry invading your ears. But it will still be only a pressing of your flesh and sounds in your head—nothing more. You can't splice your nerves into theirs and feel even a prick of their pain, a spasm of their woe.

The only pain that you can ever know is your own.

The numbers shock us, surely. Six million in the Holocaust; millions in this war, millions in that famine; tens of thousands in this flood, tens of thousands in that tsunami. But in each case, every one those thousands, of those tens of thousands, of those millions—each single person knew only his or her own pain, only his or her own suffering, and not a speck more.

LISTEN IN
visit **answrs.co/pain** to listen to a presentation that goes along with what you're reading in this chapter.

There's no sum total of human pain, because it's never totaled. No human being has ever suffered more than what a single human being can endure. Thus, in a real sense, the world has never known any more suffering than just what one single person can know, as terrible as that single person's suffering can be.

The Exception

There is, however, one exception.

Isaiah 53:4, talking about Jesus, God, on the cross, said: "Surely He has borne *our griefs*, and carried *our sorrows*." Whose griefs? Whose sorrows? According to the Bible, Christ's death was universal; it was for every human being who ever lived or would ever live. Thus, the grief and sorrow that each one of us has known personally; that is, the grief and sorrow that we ourselves alone can experience—the text is saying that God, in the person of Christ on the cross, experienced them all at once.

Read the text again: "Surely He has borne our griefs, and carried our sorrows." Our griefs, our sorrows, that which we have

WATCH visit **answrs.co/suffering** to watch a short video on why there is so much suffering in our world | 3:17

known as individuals—God has suffered them all on the cross.

The Suffering God

Thus, instead of staying up in heaven, while we struggle down here—God came down into humanity and, in ways that that we, as individuals, could never know—God Himself suffered for the sins and evils of humanity.

Why?

Because, again, so sacred was the principle of love and the freedom in love that, rather than create mindless robots who had to obey no matter what, God created us free. Though He knew beforehand what would happen, He was willing to come down, take humanity upon Himself, and suffer, corporately, what every human being can know only individually.

Sure, this amazing truth doesn't fully answer the questions. Some argue that there is no good and logical answer for evil. If there were, then it could be justified. It could be said that there's a good reason for evil, when there isn't and there

FACT ABOUT SUFFERING

At least 16.2 million adults in America (6.7%) have experienced depression in the last year.

Q&A FROM THE BIBLE

What is God?
"He who does not love does not know God, for **God is love**" (1 John 4:8).

In the parable of the wheat and the tares what question was God asked?
"So the servants of the owner came and said to him, 'Sir, did you **not sow good** seed in your field? **How then does it have tares**?'" (Matthew 13:27).

What do the good and bad seeds represent?
"The field is the world, the **good seeds are the sons of the kingdom**, but the **tares are the sons of the wicked one**" (Matthew 13:38).

What was God's answer to their question of why there was evil in the world God created?
He said to them, '**An enemy has done this**'" (Matthew 13:28).

Who is this enemy?
"The enemy who sowed them is **the devil**" (Matthew 13:39).

When God made Lucifer, the angel who became the devil, did God make him defective?
"You were **perfect in your ways** from the **day you were created**, till iniquity was found in you" (Ezekiel 28:15).

What did the servants offer to do to the tares?
"He said to them, 'An enemy has done this.' The servants said to him, 'Do you want us then to **go and gather them up**?'" (Matthew 13:28).

What was God's answer to their offer?
"But he said, '**No**'" (Matthew 13:29).

Who are these servants who work in the harvest field?
"The **reapers are the angels**" (Matthew 13:39).

Why did God not want the angels to go and destroy to bad seeds immediately?
"But he said, 'No, lest while you gather up the tares **you also uproot the wheat** with them'" (Matthew 13:29).

What do plants need time to show in order to know what they really are?
"Either make the tree good and its fruit good, or else make the tree bad and its fruit bad; for a **tree is known by its fruit**" (Matthew 12:33).

What can God do that even the angels cannot do?
"Then hear in heaven Your dwelling place, and forgive, and act, and give to everyone according to all his ways, whose heart You know (for **You alone know the hearts** of all the sons of men)" (1 Kings 8:39).

What else can God do that no other being, not even the angels, can do?
Remember the former things, those of long ago; I am God, and there is no other; I am God, and there is none like me. **I make known the end from the beginning**, from ancient times, **what is still to come**. I say, 'My purpose will stand, and I will do all that I please'" (Isaiah 46:9,10, NIV).

Since the angels cannot know the future or read the hearts of people what mistake would they make if they prematurely destroyed the people who they thought were wicked and would remain wicked?
"But he said, 'No, lest while you gather up the tares you also **uproot the wheat** with them'" (Matthew 13:29).

Since God is love, what does He give each person the privilege to do?
"And if it seems evil to you to serve the LORD, **choose for yourselves** this day **whom you will serve**, whether the gods which your

Come to Me, all you who labor and are heavy laden, and I will give you

Rest

Matthew 11:28

Q&A FROM THE BIBLE

fathers served that were on the other side of the River, or the gods of the Amorites, in whose land you dwell. But as for me and my house, we will serve the LORD" (Joshua 24:15).

Often what do we as humans tend to do with our freedom of choice?

"Then the LORD said to Moses: 'How long will **these people reject Me**? And how long will they **not believe Me**, with all the signs which I have performed among them?'" (Numbers 14:11).

What do we bring upon ourselves by choosing to reject God and the teaching He has given us?

"Because they **hated knowledge** and **did not choose** the fear of the LORD, they would have **none of my counsel** and **despised my every rebuke**. Therefore they shall eat **the fruit of their own way**, and be filled to the full **with their own fancies**" (Proverbs 1:29-31).

"Do not be deceived, God is not mocked; for **whatever a man sows**, that **he will also reap**. For he who sows to his flesh will of the flesh reap corruption, but he who sows to the Spirit will of the Spirit reap everlasting life" (Galatians 6:7, 8).

What promises does God give us that help us when we are experiencing pain and suffering?

"No temptation has overtaken you except such as is common to man; but God is faithful, who will **not allow you to be tempted beyond what you are able**, but with the temptation will also **make the way of escape**, that you may be able to bear it" (1 Corinthians 10:13).

"**Casting all your care upon Him**, for He cares for you" (1 Peter 5:7).

"For I consider that the sufferings of this present time are not worthy to be compared with the glory which shall be revealed in us. And we know that **all things work together for good** to those who love God, to those who are the called according to His purpose" (Romans 8:18, 28).

Will pain and suffering ever come to an end?

"And God will wipe away every tear from their eyes; there shall be no more death, nor sorrow, nor crying. There shall be **no more pain**, for the **former things have passed away**" (Revelation 21:4).

shouldn't be. (You want, for instance, a good reason why a six-year-old gets cancer, suffers for years in a hospital, and then dies, anyway?)

Thus, however much Fyodor Dostoyevsky, in *The Brothers Karamazov*, sought for answers about pain and suffering, he didn't find those answers. And that's because they don't exist. There's just the powerful revelation of God Himself, in Christ, bearing in Himself evil and suffering in ways that none of us ever can or will.

Hence, in the midst of all our anguish the only answer *The Answer Book* can give, is, yes—Jesus on the cross.

READ MORE + SHARE THIS TOPIC

Visit **www.glowonline.org/answer/hurting** to read more about what you just read here. You can also share it on social media.

JUDGMENT

10

"Probably No God"

Years ago, atheists in England, led by well-known writer and atheist fundamentalist Richard Dawkins, had a campaign in which the following sign appeared in blazing letters on the side of those red double-decker London buses: "There's probably no God. Now stop worrying and enjoy your life." (Notice the bit of hedging ... "probably" no God?)

If, however, they were right, and "there's probably no God," then think about what that would mean as far as the question of justice ever being done for all the evil that has been done. Any hope of justice, any hope of answers, any hope of anything to make up for all the inequities, injustice, and evil done here—evil that never seems to be accounted for—it will never come.

Evil Actions

For instance, David Berlinski wrote about the Nazi advance through Eastern Europe in World War II: "Before the possibility of Soviet retribution even entered their troubled imagination, Nazi extermination squads would sweep into villages, and after forcing villagers to dig their own graves, murder their victims with machine guns. On one such occasion somewhere in Eastern Europe, an SS officer watched languidly, his machine gun cradled, as an elderly and bearded Hasidic Jew laboriously dug what he knew to be his grave.

"Standing straight up, he addressed his executioner. 'God is watching what you are doing,' he said.

"And then he was shot dead."

Now, the question is: What happened to that officer who killed that old man and who knows how many others? Did he die a horrific death in battle, or did he survive the war and live a long and prosperous life before dying of old age?

This is just one example of, surely, billions where evil has never been answered for, and if there is "probably no God"—no God of justice and judgment—will never be answered for.

Where Is the Justice?

After all, where is the justice for the millions of Africans who, through the centuries, were torn from their homes, crammed on ships unfit for animals, carted across the seas, and forced into slavery?

WATCH visit **answrs.co/judgment** to watch a short video about the investigative judgment | 3:13

visit **answrs.co/messiah** to watch the video *The Messiah and the Judgment* | 58:30

WATCH

visit **answrs.co/criteria** to watch a video answering questions including *What are the criteria that will be used in the judgment?* **and** *Why does the sanctuary in heaven need to be cleansed if there's no sin there?*

Where is the justice for the millions Stalin killed in the Soviet Union? Or Mao killed in China? Or Pol Pot in Cambodia?

Where is the justice for millions—children, too—forced into human trafficking?

Where is the justice for the innumerable women abused and oppressed?

Where is the justice for the billions of the world's poor exploited by their leaders?

If there is "probably no God," then the answer to these questions, and all the others like them, is that this justice is nowhere to be found because it does not and never will exist.

God Is Judge

On the other hand, if the Bible teaches anything, it teaches not only that God is real but that He is a God of justice, and the justice that we do not see done here will be done in the judgment. Scripture is unequivocal: Judgment will come.

"Look, I am coming soon, bringing my reward with me to repay all people according to their deeds" (Revelation 22:12, NLT).

"God will judge us for everything we do, including every secret thing, whether good or bad" (Ecclesiastes 12:14, NLT).

"But the LORD reigns forever, executing judgment from his throne. He will judge the world with justice and rule the nations with fairness" (Psalm 9:7, 8, NLT).

"And do you think this, O man, you who judge those practicing such things, and doing the same, that you will escape the judgment of God?" (Romans 2:3, NKJV).

"But the heavens and the earth which are now preserved by the same word, are reserved for fire until the day of judgment and perdition of ungodly men" (2 Peter 3:7, NKJV).

"Fear God and give glory to Him, for the hour of His judgment has come; and worship Him who made heaven and earth, the sea and springs of water" (Revelation 14:7).

The Cross and Judgment

These texts, and many others, promise that God will bring justice; that is, the justice and judgment that we almost never see now will, indeed, be made manifest.

Nevertheless, this impending judgment does raise questions: *How will you fare in the judgment? What are your odds? What hope do you—a sinner—have?* Yes, even if you weren't engaged in child porn or drug smuggling (and maybe even if you were)—Scripture is adamant that God will bring every work into judgment, even "every secret thing" (Ecclesiastes 12:14). And, because Scripture is also adamant that we are all sinners, worthy of condemnation—*what hope do any of us have in this judgment?*

Here's, however, the good news of the gospel, of Jesus Christ's death. At the cross, God had already judged, and condemned, the world's evil. But that judgment and condemnation fell

How many will be judged by God?
"But why do you judge your brother? Or why do you show contempt for your brother? For we shall **all stand before the judgment seat** of Christ" (Romans 14:10).

Does this include the righteous?
"I said in my heart, 'God shall **judge the righteous and the wicked**, for there is a time there for every purpose and for every work'" (Ecclesiastes 3:17).

What will we be judged by?
"A fiery stream issued and came forth from before Him. A thousand thousands ministered to Him; ten thousand times ten thousand stood before Him. The court was seated, and **the books were opened**" (Daniel 7:10).

Since we are judged by these books what must be written in these books?
"For God will bring **every work into judgment**, including every secret thing, whether good or evil" (Ecclesiastes 12:14).

"And I saw the dead, small and great, standing before God, and **books were opened**. And another book was opened, which is the Book of Life. And the dead were judged **according to their works**, by the things which were **written in the books**" (Revelation 20:12).

When does this judgment begin?
"Saying with a loud voice, 'Fear God and give glory to Him, for the **hour of His judgment has come**; and worship Him who made heaven and earth, the sea and springs of water'" (Revelation 14:7).

Since judgment begins in the first angel's message, which is before the Second Coming, who does judgment begin with?
"For the time has come for judgment to **begin at the house of God**; and if it begins with us first, what will be the end of those who do not obey the gospel of God?" (1 Peter 4:17).

Why does Jesus need to examine the books before He comes back for His people?
"And behold, I am coming quickly, and **My reward is with Me**, to give to every one **according to his work**" (Revelation 22:12).

What is the standard that our lives will be evaluated by in the judgment?
"For whoever shall keep the **whole law**, and yet stumble in one point, he is guilty of all. For He who said, '**Do not commit adultery**,' also said, '**Do not murder**.' Now if you do not commit adultery, but you do murder, you have become a transgressor of the law. So speak and so do as those who will be judged by the **law of liberty**" (James 2:10-12).

on Jesus; Jesus faced the punishment for evil, a judgment that only a righteous God could justly bring. Describing Jesus on the cross, the Bible says: "All we like sheep have gone astray; We have turned, every one, to his own way; And the LORD has laid on Him the iniquity of us all" (Isaiah 53:6).

Yes, the good news is that instead of condemnation falling on us, we who deserve it, Jesus took it, "the inequity of us all," upon Himself—the just for the unjust, the righteous for the unrighteous, the innocent for the guilty. The great provision of the gospel is that any person, who, by faith, claims what Jesus has done for them, is automatically pardoned.

LISTEN IN visit **answrs.co/court** to listen to a presentation that goes along with what you're reading in this chapter.

How many have sinned and fallen short of keeping God's law?

"As it is written: 'There is **none righteous**, no, not one; There is none who understands; There is none who seeks after God. They have all turned aside; They have together become unprofitable; There is none who does good, **no, not one**'" (Romans 3:10-12).

"For **all have sinned** and fall short of the glory of God" (Romans 3:23).

Is there hope since we have sinned and broken God's perfect law?

"Who Himself **bore our sins in His own body** on the tree, that we, having died to sins, might live for righteousness—by whose stripes you were healed" (1 Peter 2:24).

"If we **confess our sins**, He is faithful and just to **forgive us our sins** and to **cleanse us** from all unrighteousness" (1 John 1:9).

"I have **blotted out**, like a thick cloud, **your transgressions**, and like a cloud, your sins. Return to Me, for I have redeemed you" (Isaiah 44:22).

What will the saints inherit after this judgment has ended?

"'But the **court shall be seated**, and they shall take away his dominion, to consume and destroy it forever. **Then the kingdom and dominion**, and the greatness of the kingdoms under the whole heaven, **shall be given to the people, the saints of the Most High**. His kingdom is an everlasting kingdom, and all dominions shall serve and obey Him" (Daniel 7:26, 27).

Who is the judge in the heavenly court?

"For the Father judges no one, but has **committed all judgment to the Son**" (John 5:22).

Who is going to advocate our case in this Heavenly court?

"My little children, these things I write to you, so that you may not sin. And if anyone sins, **we have an Advocate** with the Father, **Jesus Christ the righteous**" (1 John 2:1).

Since the judge is also in a sense our lawyer who will defend us what will be the outcome of our case if we choose Jesus to daily stand by our side?

"For the LORD is **our Judge**, the LORD is **our Lawgiver**, the LORD is **our King**; He will **save us**" (Isaiah 33:22).

Who is this judgment in favor of?

"Until the Ancient of Days came, and a judgment was made **in favor of the saints** of the Most High, and the time came for the saints to possess the kingdom" (Daniel 7:22).

At the cross, God's justice and grace were both made manifest: His justice because He punished all evil and His grace because He punished all that evil in Jesus, so we don't have to face it ourselves.

Yes, final judgment is coming. The world will have to answer for its evil. But, thanks to Jesus, everyone can find pardon and forgiveness. On the other hand, if "there's probably no God," then there's hope of nothing but eternal death, unpunished injustice, and unanswered evil.

READ MORE + SHARE THIS TOPIC
Visit **www.glowonline.org/answer/judgment** to read more about what you just read here. You can also share it on social media.

11

DEATH

I See Dead People!

Every now and then, some Hollywood flick creates an iconic line that makes it into everyday language and becomes, to use a modern phrase, a meme.

Like:

"I'm going to make him an offer he can't refuse."

"Go ahead, make my day."

"Toto, I've got a feeling we're not in Kansas anymore…"

And—"I see dead people!"

That last line, about seeing dead people, was from M. Night Shyamalan's *The Sixth Sense*, which became an international phenomenon as it took advantage of the human fascination with, and fear of, death.

The Dead

No matter who we are, how rich, or famous, or beautiful—it makes no difference. Death gets us all.

Thus, the natural question is: *What happens to the dead?*

Many think that death is a transition into another realm; that is, humans possess an immortal soul which floats off into another existence. Even many Christians believe that the soul at death immediately goes either to heaven or to hell. On the other hand, some Christians believe that the dead are unconscious in the grave until Christ returns, and only then are they resurrected to eternal life.

What, then, does the Bible teach? What does it say about the dead: immediate reward (or punishment) at death, or an unconscious sleep until the resurrection?

Jesus Speaks About Death

To begin, here's Jesus Himself speaking on the topic of the dead:

"Do not marvel at this; for the hour is coming in which all who are in the graves will hear His voice and come forth—those who have done good, to the resurrection of life, and those who have done evil, to the resurrection of condemnation" (John 5:28, 29, NKJV).

Does this sound as if the dead have gone immediately to their reward or punishment? Or as if they sleep in the grave, awaiting judgment? Christ's words do sound very much like the latter; in fact, the words make no sense otherwise.

The Dead Asleep

Or how about this text from the Old Testament?

"Many of those whose bodies lie dead and

WATCH visit **answrs.co/death** to watch a short video on what the Bible teaches about death | 3:17

WATCH visit **answrs.co/hope** to watch

the video *The Mystery of Death* | 58:31

buried will rise up, some to everlasting life and some to shame and everlasting disgrace" (Daniel 12: 2, NLT).

What is this verse talking about if the dead were already being rewarded or punished as soon as they died? The text teaches that they are dead and buried awaiting their final destiny.

What do the following texts mean if, indeed, the dead are already either in heaven or in hell?

"The living at least know they will die, but the dead know nothing. They have no further reward, nor are they remembered" (Ecclesiastes 9:5, NLT).

"When they breathe their last, they return to the earth, and all their plans die with them" (Psalm 146:4, NLT).

"The dead cannot sing praises to the LORD,

for they have gone into the silence of the grave" (Psalm 115:17, NLT).

It's hard to square these verses with the common notion, even among many Christians, that at death the deceased go straight into another conscious existence. In contrast, these texts make perfect sense if the dead are unconscious in the ground, asleep until the resurrection.

Paul on Death

Meanwhile, responding to those who denied the idea of the resurrection of the dead, the apostle Paul linked the resurrection of Jesus to the end-time resurrection of the dead, writing:

"And if Christ has not been raised, then your faith is useless and you are still guilty of your sins. In that case, all who have died believing in Christ are lost!" (1 Corinthians 15:17, 18, NLT).

Those fallen asleep in Christ, that is, the Christians who have died, are lost if there's no resurrection? Why? Aren't the dead already in heaven with Jesus now?

If, however, the dead are asleep, unconscious in the grave, the text is easily explainable. If there's no end-time resurrection of the dead, then the dead stay dead, forever, which is why Paul said that their faith would be "useless." After all, what good is belief in Jesus if you die and rot forever in the ground?

Near Death or *Real* Death?

Most everyone has heard of Near Death Experiences (NDEs). This is when people "die," are revived, and then tell of extraordinary things that they believe happened to them while dead.

What do we do with these stories?

First, these people are only *near* death, not dead dead, as in embalmed, cremated, or *rigor mortis* dead. They all came back to life, which should if nothing else make us cautious about what someone who had experienced only a near death can reveal about real death.

Also, what better way for the supernatural powers, hostile supernatural

LISTEN IN visit **answrs.co/sleep** to listen to a presentation that goes along with what you're reading in this chapter.

FACT ABOUT DEATH

After death, the baterial cells living on and in a human body multiply and begin to break it down, eventually making it just dust.

pow- ers (see chapter nine), who don't want people to believe in Jesus, to cause people to doubt than to give them experiences about an afterlife that has nothing to do with Jesus? Many who had NDEs were not Christians, and they recount-

ed meeting various beings or presences who they believed were other dead people, angels, or even God. And yet, these personalities and presences, instead of giving them any biblical truth, usually uttered sweet platitudes about goodness, love, and kindness—all which is fine, but these are not distinctly Christian virtues. That is, the supernatural beings had nothing to say to them about sin, salvation, and the need of Jesus as Savior, distinct Christian teachings.

"One would think," writes one author about NDEs, "that while these people were supposedly getting a taste of the Christian afterlife, they

Q&A FROM THE BIBLE

What do we all know will eventually happen to us?
"For the living **know** that they will **die**" (Ecclesiastes 9:5)

In order to understand death we need to know our creation. According to the creation account what is man?
"And the LORD God formed man of the dust of the ground, and breathed into his nostrils the breath of life; and man **became a living soul**" (Genesis 2:7, KJV)

What two components make up man, which is a living soul?
"And the LORD God formed man of the **dust of the ground**, and breathed into his nostrils the **breath of life**; and man **became** a living **soul**" (Genesis 2:7, KJV)

Since a soul is our body plus our breath then can a soul die?
"Behold, all souls are Mine; the soul of the father as well as the soul of the son is Mine; the **soul** who sins **shall die**" (Ezekiel 18:4)

If our "soul" is able to die then who is immortal?
"...He who is the blessed and only Potentate, the King of kings and Lord of lords, who **alone has immortality**, dwelling in unapproachable light, whom no man has seen or can see, to whom be honor and everlasting power. Amen" (1 Timothy 6:15, 16).

What do people know after they die?
"For the living know that they will die; but the **dead know nothing**" (Ecclesiastes 9:5).

In death do we remember who God is?
"Return, O LORD, deliver me! Oh, save me for Your mercies' sake! For in death there is **no remembrance of You**; In the grave who will give You thanks?" (Psalm 6:4,5).

would have gotten a taste of Christian truth as well. But that rarely, if ever, happens."

In fact, many who have had NDEs come away less inclined toward Christianity than they were before the experience. After all, if there's something inherently immortal in us, which means that we will live forever because that's how we were made, then who needs Jesus and the plan of salvation? If NDEs are, truly, what these people think that they are, we have eternal life already.

The Second Coming

Death is real, as real as life, unfortunately. The good news of the gospel, however, is that because of Christ's sacrifice, death does not have to have the last word. Through His own sacrifice, Jesus promises anyone who claims Him by faith the opportunity to partake in eternal life.

"Look, I am coming soon, bringing my

Q&A: Death

WATCH

visit **answrs.co/paradise** to watch a video answering questions including *Didn't Jesus tell the thief on the cross that He would be with him in paradise that day? Didn't Paul say that to be absent from the body is to be present with the Lord?* **And** *Where do you go immediately after taking your last breath?*

Do people praise God after they die?
"The dead do not praise the LORD, nor any who go down into silence" (Psalm 115:17).

Do those who die still participate with events or interact with living people?
"Also their love, their hatred, and their envy have now perished; nevermore will they have a **share in anything done under the sun**" (Ecclesiastes 9:6).

If the dead remember nothing, don't praise God, nor give God thanks for what He has done then what does the Bible say the dead are doing?
"But man dies and is laid away; indeed he breathes his last and where is he…So man lies down and does not rise. Till the heavens are no more, they will not **awake** nor be roused from their **sleep**" (Job 14:10, 12).

"Now the days of David drew near that he should **die**, … So David **rested** with his fathers, and was buried in the City of David" (1 Kings 2:1, 10).

Where are the Bible heroes, like King David, at today?
"Men and brethren, let me speak freely to you of the patriarch David, that he is both **dead** and **buried**, and his **tomb** is with us **to this day** … For David did not ascend into the heavens" (Acts 2:29, 34).

How did Jesus speak about death?
"These things He said, and after that He said to them, 'Our friend Lazarus **sleeps**, but I go that I may **wake him up**.' Then His disciples said, 'Lord, if he sleeps he will get well.' However, Jesus **spoke of his death**, but they thought that He was speaking about **taking rest in sleep**. Then Jesus said to them plainly, 'Lazarus is **dead**'" (John 11:11-14).

Why is it important to know that the dead are sleeping and not awake somewhere interacting with the living?
"Now the Spirit expressly says that in latter times some will depart from the faith, giving heed to deceiving spirits and doctrines of demons" (1 Timothy 4:1).

"For they are spirits of demons, performing signs, which go out to the kings of the earth and of the whole world, to gather them to the battle of that great day of God Almighty" (Revelation 16:14).

"And no wonder! For Satan himself transforms himself into an angel of light" (2 Corinthians 11:14).

Will the dead ever come back to life?
"Behold, I tell you a mystery: We shall not all sleep, but we shall all be changed—in a moment, in the twinkling of an eye, at the last trumpet. For the trumpet will sound, and the dead will be raised incorruptible, and we shall be changed. For this corruptible must put on incorruption, and this mortal must put on immortality" (1 Corinthians 15:51-53).

"For the Lord Himself will descend from heaven with a shout, with the voice of an archangel, and with the trumpet of God. And the dead in Christ will rise first. Then we who are alive and remain shall be caught up together with them in the clouds to meet the Lord in the air. And thus we shall always be with the Lord. Therefore comfort one another with these words" (1 Thessalonians 4:16-18).

FACT ABOUT DEATH

The Bible refers to death as a sleep more than 30 times. These references appear in both the Old Testament as well as the New Testament.

reward with me to repay all people according to their deeds " (Revelation 22:12).

Jesus is bringing His reward with Him? What is He talking about if the faithful dead get their reward immediately at death, soaring off to heaven? On the other hand, if the dead are asleep, unconscious in the grave until the resurrection at Christ's return, Jesus' promise here makes perfect sense (Ecclesiastes 9:5).

Yes, thanks to Jesus, "The last enemy to be destroyed is death" (1 Corinthians 15:26, NIV). This means that, when Christ returns, "the trumpet will sound, the dead will be raised imperishable, and we will be changed. For the perishable must clothe itself with the imperishable, and the mortal with immortality. When the perishable has been clothed with the imperishable, and the mortal with immortality, then the saying that is written will come true: 'Death has been swallowed up in victory'" (1 Corinthians 15: 52-54, NIV).

Thus, when people say something similar to what the boy in *The Sixth Sense* said, "I see dead people!" we can be sure that whatever they saw, it wasn't, indeed, dead people.

DEATH'S SILENT TRUTH

Giving Light to Our World

READ MORE + SHARE THIS TOPIC

Visit **www.glowonline.org/answer/death** to read more about what you just read here. You can also share it on social media.

HELL

12

Miners in Siberia, as they drilled deep, began hearing strange noises. Cries and screams of agony. Horrified, they realized that they had drilled into hell itself, and the sounds were of people burning there.

Don't believe it? Get on YouTube and you can, with your own ears, hear it for yourself!

Fact or Fiction

No rational person is, of course, going to believe that story. Nevertheless, an incredible numbers of false teachings exist regarding hell; perhaps the most widespread, egregious and damaging is that people will be tortured there for eternity.

A worldwide influencial leader, Pope Benedict XVI, in 2007, said that hell is real, and that people burn there forever. At the time, a headline from *The Times* of London online read: "The Fires of Hell are real and eternal, Pope warns." Not only were they real, but he was quoted as saying that hell "really exists and is eternal, even if nobody talks about it much anymore."

One of the most enduring pictures of the fate awaiting the damned came from the fourteenth century poet, Dante, whose *Divine Comedy* depicts hell as a series of nine underground levels, circles—each one deeper and deeper under the earth as the torment gets worse and worse. Which circle you end up in depends on how badly you sinned. The most famous part of the poem is the beginning, which depicts a sign at the entrance to hell, which reads: "Abandon all hope, ye who enter here."

Like the miners supposedly hearing the sounds of those in hell, Dante's poem was fiction. The problem, however, is that much of what is commonly taught about hell is fiction, too.

Whatever fate awaits the dead, it's going to last a lot longer than their earthly life here. In other words, we're dead a lot longer than we are alive, right? Wouldn't it, then, be in our best interest to know what really happens after death, short term and long term, especially when the long term is, well, eternally long?

A Quick Review

As we saw in the chapter on death, the dead (at least short term) are asleep, unconscious until the end time. Here are just a couple of refresher texts:

"His breath goes forth, he returns to his earth; in that very day his thoughts

WATCH

visit **answrs.co/hell** to see a short video about hell fire

2:31

perish" (Psalm 146:4, KJV).

"For the living know that they shall die: but the dead know not any thing" (Ecclesiastes 9:5, KJV).

"The dead praise not the LORD, neither any that go down into silence" (Psalm 115:17, KJV).

One thing is sure, then: The dead, even the ones most vile while alive, don't immediately get thrown into one of Dante's nine circles of hell. No, the dead—the good and the bad—sleep until judgment day.

Hell to Pay

Now, just because the dead, even the evil dead, sleep, this doesn't mean that they will do so forever. As we saw in chapter 10, if the Bible teaches anything, it teaches that there will be a final judgment, and that the evil unpunished here will, indeed, be punished in that judgment.

Yes, there will be—for many—hell to pay.

The question is, and this gets to the heart of the whole issue of hell itself—What is the nature of God's ultimate punishment of the wicked?

Two Eternal Fates

Everyone has probably heard what's, perhaps, the most famous Bible text ever:

"For God so loved the world that He gave His only begotten Son, that whoever believes in Him should not perish but have everlasting life" (John 3:16).

How many fates, how many options, are depicted here? Two. One is "everlasting life," while the other is ... what? To be tormented in fire forever and ever? That's not what the text says, not even close. It seems, rather, to say the opposite, because to burn forever means you

LISTEN IN visit **answrs.co/torment** to listen to a presentation that goes along with what you're reading in this chapter.

Q&A FROM THE BIBLE

What will happen to the wicked who reject God's free gift of salvation?
"But the cowardly, unbelieving, abominable, murderers, sexually immoral, sorcerers, idolaters, and all liars shall **have their part in the lake which burns with fire** and brimstone, which is the **second death**" (Revelation 21:8).

Was this lake of fire experience originally intended for humans to experience or someone else?
"Then He will also say to those on the left hand, 'Depart from Me, you cursed, into the everlasting fire **prepared for the devil** and his angels'" (Matthew 25:41).

Where does the lake of fire experience take place?
"They went up on the **breadth of the earth** and surrounded the camp of the saints and the beloved city. And **fire came down** from God out of heaven **and devoured them**" (Revelation 20:9).

What eventually happens to the wicked?
"'For behold, the day is coming, burning like an oven, and all the proud, yes, all who do wickedly **will be stubble**. And the day which is coming shall **burn them up**,' says the LORD of hosts, 'That will leave them neither root nor branch...You shall trample the wicked, for they shall be **ashes** under the soles of your feet on the day that I do this,' Says the LORD of hosts'" (Malachi 4:1,3).

"But the **wicked shall perish**; and the enemies of the LORD, like the splendor of the meadows, shall vanish. **Into smoke they shall vanish away**" (Psalm 37:20).

must exist forever. But according to the verse, those who don't face everlasting life face… what? They "perish." Perish, as in being destroyed. Perish, as in annihilation.

Hell is real. The punishment is real. The fire is real. It's just not eternal, that's all. The punishment, not the punishing, lasts forever. In contrast to those who through the grace of Jesus face eternal life, those who rejected the grace of Jesus face eternal destruction.

There are two eternal fates: eternal life, or its opposite, eternal destruction.

Here's Jesus again: "Do not fear those who kill the body but are unable to kill the soul; but

WATCH visit **answrs.co/lake** to watch the video
Revelation's Lake of Fire | 58:31

Will this experience last forever since it is an eternal fire?

"As **Sodom and Gomorrah**, and the cities around them in a similar manner to these, having given themselves over to sexual immorality and gone after strange flesh, are set forth as **an example**, suffering the vengeance of **eternal fire**" (Jude 7).

"And **turning** the cities of **Sodom and Gomorrah into ashes**, condemned them to destruction, making them **an example** to those who afterward would live ungodly" (2 Peter 2:6).

When will the wicked experience the second death?

"Do not marvel at this; for the hour is coming in which all who are in the **graves** will **hear His voice** and **come forth**—those who have done good, to the resurrection of life, and those who have **done evil**, to the **resurrection of condemnation**" (John 5:28,29).

When will this resurrection occur?

"Now **when the thousand years have expired**, Satan will be released from his prison and will go out to deceive the nations which are in the four corners of the earth, Gog and Magog, to gather them together to battle, whose number is as the sand of the sea. They went up on the breadth of the earth and surrounded the camp of the saints and the beloved city. And fire came down from God out of heaven and devoured them" (Revelation 20:7-9).

Does God enjoy destroying people?

"Say to them: 'As I live,' says the Lord GOD, 'I have **no pleasure in the death of the wicked**, but that the wicked turn from his way and live. Turn, turn from your evil ways! For why should you die, O house of Israel?'" (Ezekiel 33:11).

rather fear Him who is able to destroy both soul and body in hell" (Matthew 10:28, NASB).

If we let the text speak, what does it say? It says to fear the one who is able to destroy both the body and the soul in hell (not put them over a barbecue where they sizzle and simmer and scream forever). Thus, here's Jesus Himself showing that the soul, like the body, is not immortal but will, indeed, be destroyed in hell.

Talking about the lost, those who will face hell, the apostle Paul writes: "Who shall be punished with everlasting destruction from the presence of the Lord, and from the glory of his power" (2 Thessalonians 1:9, KJV).

What do they face? Everlasting torture? Everlasting burning? Everlasting suffering? No, everlasting destruction. The result (destruction), not the process leading to the result, is everlasting.

And that's a distinction that makes a big difference.

The Justice of It All

Yes, God will bring justice, the justice that we don't see here. We have been promised that He will (see chapter 10). But what kind of justice would it be for God to torture for eternity, for billions of years, people who have lived here for only twenty, forty, even ninety years? A thousand billion centuries of torture in hell for whatever sins they committed here? And that's only the beginning of their punishment?

If true, that would be as bad, even worse, than the injustices we see now.

But what about texts that talk about eternal fire, and so forth?

WATCH

visit **answrs.co/forever** to watch a video answering questions including *How do you know that hell doesn't burn forever if the Bible says "forever"? Can you explain the story of Saul and the Witch of Endor?* **And** *If hellfire is unquenchable, how can it go out?*

Though we don't have space here, a quick look at those texts, and the biblical use of the word "forever," shows that they refer to something that is completed, finished, as opposed to eternal. Jonah, in the belly of the big fish for three days, said, "The earth with its bars closed behind me forever" (Jonah 2:6). Forever?

In numerous places in the Bible, when it talks about God bringing judgment upon a place, such as Jerusalem, it talks about Him destroying the place with a fire that shall "not be quenched" (Jeremiah 7:20). A fire not quenched? Does that mean it's burning forever? It doesn't appear so. Instead, it's biblical language that gives the idea of completion, of fulfillment; it means that the fire will do its work and nothing can stop it.

Hell will do the same thing. It will burn until everything is destroyed, forever.

A Choice to Make

None of us asked to be born; we were brought here, not of our own choice. We came out of nothingness, too. Then, due to sin, things went

FACT ABOUT HELL

The fires of hell are real, but they don't exist today and won't last for all of eternity.

badly, very badly. However, through the death of Jesus on the cross, God offers us all one of two choices. Eternal life with Him in a new heaven and a new earth, like the paradise that He first created. Or, we can go back to the nothingness from which we first arose. That's the truth about hell–God allowing us to return to the nothing

from which we came.

One of these two fates, two eternal fates, will be ours. Which one will we receive? Well, the one we choose.

READ MORE + SHARE THIS TOPIC

Visit **www.glowonline.org/answer/hell** to read more about what you just read here. You can also share it on social media.

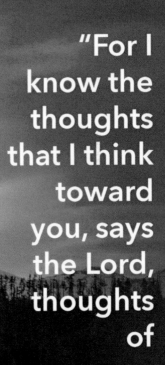

"For I know the thoughts that I think toward you, says the Lord, thoughts of

Peace

and not of evil, to give you a future and a hope."

Jeremiah 29:11

PROPHECY

13

Making an Accurate Prediction

Those alive in the last half of the twentieth century lived amid the Cold War. The United States and the Soviet Union, each armed and ready to annihilate the other, dominated the geo-political atmosphere for decades.

Though many experts speculated about what would happen between the superpowers, the reality of what did happen surprised everyone. The Soviet Union, this world empire—nuclear-armed to the teeth—just collapsed. Having spent billions of dollars on surveillance and cloak-and-dagger spy craft against the Soviet Union for decades, Western intelligence agencies still did not see this fall coming.

One U.S. intelligence analyst, who watched as the Soviet empire disintegrated before his eyes, uttered: "Our jaws were dropping in astonishment. We never expected this, ever!"

No wonder a scientist once quipped: "It's very difficult to make an accurate prediction—especially about the future."

Bible Prophecy

As anyone who has ever tried knows, predicting the future isn't easy. Though weathermen, using sophisticated computers, satellites, and the latest technology, do fine, they still don't always get it right. And that's even with something like the weather, which follows basic natural laws that can be expressed with math formulas.

How much more difficult does predicting the future get when it involves human behavior? Humans often can't give rational answers for the choices that they make because the choices that they make are, indeed, often not rational. Millions of dollars, for example, are lost every day in the stock market because people, thinking they know what others will do, get it wrong.

Telling the future is hard, yes. Yet, there are many prophecies in the Bible that make accurate predictions about events hundreds, even thousands, of years in advance. The outcomes of these prophecies are precisely why they can provide powerful evidence for trusting in the Bible as the Word of God.

What are some of these biblical prophecies, and how do they show us that, first, God knows the future, and, second, we can trust in Him because He knows the future?

Daniel 2

One of the most wide-ranging prophecies is found in Daniel chapter 2, written more than 500 years before Christ. This prophecy predicted

Q&A: Prophecy

WATCH visit **answrs.co/before** to watch a video answering questions including *How do we know that the prophecies of Daniel were written down before they happened?* and *How can you know whether or not you are interpreting prophecies correctly?*

WATCH visit **answrs.co/prophecy** to watch a short video about prophecy | 2:41

will not adhere to one another, just as iron does not mix with clay" (Daniel 2:42, 43).

Think carefully about these few lines. Western Europe, for almost all its history, has been made of powers, some which were strong, like France, Spain, England, and Germany; others that were weak (in comparison), like Belgium, Luxembourg, and Holland. Even to this day, modern Europe has some nations that are strong, militarily and financially, and others that are weak.

Even more amazing, the prophecy said that they will "mingle with the seed of men; but they will not adhere to one another." In other words, even though there will be royal marriages, or even intermarriage between commoners, these various nations of Europe will never be fully united.

Europe united? It seems unlikely, to say the least. Two world wars were fought in the last century alone seeking to keep European nations from killing each other off! To this day, Europe seems on the edge of fracturing.

the rise and fall of great empires. It told about a statue made of various metals, each a symbol of a different empire that would come and go. The head of gold was Babylon; the arms and chest of silver represented Media-Persia; the belly and thighs of brass symbolized Greece; its legs were of iron, a symbol of pagan Rome; and its feet were of iron and clay, a symbol of the breakup of the ancient Roman Empire into the nations of modern Europe today.

All these world empires came and went, exactly as Daniel had predicted. What we see today in Western Europe, which arose out of the rubble of Rome, fits exactly what Daniel had written about it 2500 years ago.

Of the feet and toes, part of iron and part of clay, Daniel made this astonishing prediction: "And as the toes of the feet were partly of iron and partly of clay, so the kingdom shall be partly strong and partly fragile. As you saw iron mixed with ceramic clay, they will mingle with the seed of men; but they

LISTEN IN
visit **answrs.co/future** to listen to a presentation that goes along with what you're reading in this chapter.

Q&A FROM THE BIBLE

What is God able to do in relation to the future?
"Behold, the former things have come to pass, and new things I declare; **before they spring forth I tell you of them**" (Isaiah 42:9).

What are the three reasons why God gives prophecies in the Bible?
"Remember the former things of old: for I am **God**, and there is **none else**; I am God, and there is none like me, **Declaring the end from the beginning**, and from ancient times the things that are not yet done, saying, My counsel shall stand, and I will do all my pleasure" (Isaiah 46:9,10).

"And now I have told you before it comes, that when it does come to pass, **you may believe**" (John 14:29).

"And so we have the prophetic word confirmed, which you do well to heed as a light that shines in a dark place, until the day dawns and the **morning star rises** in your **hearts**" (2 Peter 1:19).

Who is the morning star that rises in your hearts?
"I, **Jesus**, have sent My angel to testify to you these things in the churches. I am the Root and the Offspring of David, the Bright and **Morning Star**" (Revelation 22:16).

How much of the Bible, like prophecy, did God give intending for it to reveal Jesus?
"You search the Scriptures, for in them you think you have eternal life; and these are they which **testify of Me** [Jesus]" (John 5:39).

Will the Lord do anything to us without first giving us a warning?
"Surely the Lord GOD does **nothing**, unless He **reveals** His secret to His servants the prophets" (Amos 3:7).

Which book of the Bible speaks directly about what will happen in the future?
"Write the things which you have seen, and the things which are, and the **things** which will **take place after this**" (**Revelation** 1:19)

Which other book of the Bible contains prophecies intended for us to understand today?
"But you, **Daniel**, shut up the words, and seal the book **until the time of the end**; many shall run to and fro, and knowledge shall increase" (Daniel 12:4)

What prophecy is given in Daniel 2 as the foundational prophecy to the rest of the book of Daniel?
"You, O king, were watching; and behold, **a great image**! This great image, whose splendor was excellent, stood before you; and its form was awesome. This image's **head** was **of fine gold**, its **chest and arms of silver**, its **belly and thighs of bronze**, its **legs of iron**, its **feet partly of iron and partly of clay**. You watched while a **stone** was cut out without hands, which struck the image **on its feet** of iron and clay, and broke them in pieces. Then the iron, the clay, the bronze, the silver, and the gold were crushed together, and **became like chaff** from the summer threshing floors; the wind carried them away so that **no trace of them was found**. And the **stone** that struck the image **became a great mountain and filled the whole earth**" (Daniel 2:31-35)

What do these different metals represent?
"But after you shall arise **another kingdom** inferior to yours; then another, a third kingdom of bronze, which shall rule over all the earth. And the **fourth kingdom** shall be as strong as **iron**" (Daniel 2:39,40).

All this predicted 500 years before Christ? When the United States intelligence agencies couldn't see the fall of the Soviet Union one year before it collapsed, Daniel's track record of predicting the future is astonishing.

Other Prophecies

Scripture is filled with prophecies, prophecies about events that were predicted way before the events ultimately happened. This enables us—living after both the prediction and the fulfillment of the prediction—to see that, yes, the Bible can and does predict the future.

Jesus gave a principle that can help us understand how prophecy works. "But these things I have told you," He said, "that when the time comes, you may remember that I told you of them" (John 16:4). In other words, predictions were made before the event happened so that,

WATCH visit **answrs.co/usa** to watch the video *The United States in Bible Prophecy* | 58:31

when it did happen, we can remember that we had already been told that it would.

For example, more than 500 years before the birth of Christ, the prophet Isaiah, in chapter 53, wrote of Christ's suffering on the cross: that is, He depicted, in astonishing detail, specific events that wouldn't happen until more than half a millennium later. That would be the equivalent of someone in the 1500s making an astonishing detailed prediction about an even happening in our day!

Or consider Daniel chapter 9, again about 500 years before Christ, that gave a prophecy predicting the exact dates of Christ's ministry and crucifixion, a prophecy that over the millennia has helped millions believe that Jesus is the Messiah.

Or Psalm chapter 22, written about 900 before Christ, that amazingly describes Christ's experience on the cross, including this following verse: "They pierced My hands and feet" (Psalm 22:16).

These are just a few of many prophecies in the Bible that, if studied carefully, provide overwhelming evidence, not only of Scripture's inspiration but also of God's power and love and care for us.

THE IMAGE OF DANIEL 2:
HISTORY CONFIRMS PROPHECY

HEAD OF GOLD
Babylon
605 - 539 B.C.

CHEST & ARMS OF SILVER
Medo-Persia
539 - 331 B.C.

BELLY & THIGHS OF BRONZE
Greece
331 - 168 B.C.

LEGS OF IRON
Rome
168 B.C. - A.D. 476

FEET OF IRON & CLAY
Divided Rome
A.D. 476 - Present

The Odds in Our Favor

Oh, yes, lest we forget. There's was one more prediction in Daniel chapter 2 that we haven't looked at. According to Daniel, one more "kingdom" would arise after the others. Daniel wrote that during the time of what we see as modern Europe, in other words, the time we're living in now—"the God of heaven will set up a kingdom which shall never be destroyed; and the kingdom shall not be left to other people; it shall break in pieces and consume all these kingdoms, and it shall stand forever" (Daniel 2:44).

The point? Babylon came and went, as predicted. That's one for one. Media-Persia came and went, as predicted. That's two for two. Greece came and went as predicted. Daniel's three for three now. Pagan Rome arose and then divided, as predicted. Four for four. The nations of modern Europe arose and exist, to this day, in the form as outlined by Daniel; that is, just as predicted.

Q&A FROM THE BIBLE

Since these metals represent kingdoms, which kingdom does the head of gold represent?
"But there is a God in heaven who reveals secrets, and He has made known to **King Nebuchadnezzar** what will be in the latter days. **Your dream**, and the visions of **your head upon your bed**, were these…you are this head of gold" (Daniel 2:28,38).

"In the third year of the reign of Jehoiakim king of Judah, Nebuchadnezzar **king of Babylon** came to Jerusalem and besieged it" (Daniel 1:1).

What would happen after Babylon?
"But **after you shall arise another kingdom** inferior to yours" (Daniel 2:39).

Which kingdom comes after Babylon and is represented by the chest and arms of silver?
"In the same hour the fingers of a man's hand appeared and wrote opposite the lampstand on the plaster of the wall of the king's palace; and the king saw the part of the hand that wrote. The king cried aloud to bring in the astrologers, the Chaldeans, and the soothsayers. The king spoke, saying to the **wise men of Babylon**, 'Whoever reads this writing, and tells me its interpretation, shall be clothed with purple and have a chain of gold around his neck; and he shall be the third ruler in the kingdom'" (Daniel 5:5, 7).

"And this is the inscription that was written: MENE, MENE, TEKEL, UPHARSIN. This is the interpretation of each word. MENE: God has numbered your kingdom, and **finished it**; TEKEL: You have been weighed in the balances, and **found wanting**; PERES: Your kingdom has been divided, and **given to the Medes and Persians**" (Daniel 5:25-28).

What would happen after the Medo-Perisan empire?
"But after you shall arise another kingdom inferior to yours; **then another, a third kingdom of bronze**, which shall rule over all the earth" (Daniel 2:39).

What is this bronze kingdom that will arise to power after the Medo-Persian empire?
"I saw in the vision…Then I lifted my eyes and saw, and there, standing beside the river, was **a ram which had two horns** … I saw the ram pushing westward, northward, and southward, so that no animal could withstand him. And as I was considering, suddenly **a male goat came from the west**, across the surface of the whole earth, without touching the ground; and the goat had a notable horn between his

Daniel, then, has so far been right five out of five times. The only kingdom, from our time perspective today, that has not yet come is the last one, God's eternal kingdom, which "shall stand forever."

The Bible, thousands of years ago, was correct on each of these predictions so far. Five out of five! With all this powerful evidence before us, evidence as firm as world history and contemporary events—why not trust it on the last one, God's eternal kingdom?

The odds are, clearly, in favor of those who do.

READ MORE + SHARE THIS TOPIC

Visit **www.glowonline.org/answer/prophecy** to read more about what you just read here. You can also share it on social media.

eyes. Then **he came to the ram** that had two horns, which I had seen standing beside the river, **and ran at him with furious power**. And I saw him confronting the ram; he was moved with rage against him, **attacked the ram, and broke his two horns**. There was no power in the ram to withstand him, but he cast him down to the ground and trampled him; and there was no one that could deliver the ram from his hand" (Daniel 8:1-7).

"**The ram** which you saw, having the two horns—they **are the kings of Media and Persia**. And the **male goat** is the **kingdom of Greece**. The large horn that is between its eyes is the first king" (Daniel 8:20, 21).

How much of the known earth did the kingdom of Greece conquer?
"...then another, a third kingdom of bronze, which **shall rule over all the earth**" (Daniel 2:39).

Which kingdom do we see next in the Bible that rules all the world and therefore conquered Greece?
"And it came to pass in those days that a decree went out from **Caesar Augustus** that **all the world** should be **registered**" (Luke 2:1).

After Rome becomes a world power what does the Bible prophecy will happen to this kingdom?

"Whereas you saw the feet and toes, partly of potter's clay and partly of iron, **the kingdom shall be divided**; yet the strength of the iron shall be in it, just as you saw the iron mixed with ceramic clay" (Daniel 2:41).

Will the divided Roman Empire ever come back together like it was before?
"As you saw iron mixed with ceramic clay, they will mingle with the seed of men; **but they will not adhere to one another**, just as iron does not mix with clay" (Daniel 2:43).

What does the stone represent?
"And in the days of these kings the God of heaven will **set up a kingdom which shall never be destroyed**; and the kingdom shall not be left to other people; **it shall break in pieces and consume all these kingdoms**, and it shall **stand forever**" (Daniel 2:44).

At what event will this kingdom be established?
"When the **Son of Man comes in His glory**, and all the holy angels with Him, then He will sit on the **throne of His glory**" (Matthew 25:31).

What will this new kingdom be like?
"And God will wipe away every tear from their eyes; there shall be no more death, nor sorrow, nor crying. There shall be no more pain, for the former things have passed away" (Revelation 21:4).

14

THE SABBATH

The Tyranny of Time Theory

Some of us are old enough to remember when, in order to make a phone call, you had to stick your finger in a hole in a disc and rotate it. Seven times. And when making a long-distance call, you had to rotate it ten times! Even worse, if dialing the numbers 8, 9, or 0, you had to make almost a complete 360 turn.

In contrast, our experience today tells us that as quick as one says, "Hey, Siri, call Joe," the call is already being made.

Speed Demons

There's no question that we can get things done a lot quicker now than in days gone by. Your three-year-old desktop computer works at speeds that, 50 years ago, a computer the size of an SUV couldn't reach. Remember when the first computers stunned us with a one-megahertz CPU; that is, one million computations a second? A million per second! What has God wrought?

Today, instead of millions per second, the average home computer has CPUs that compute in the billions per second. Who knows how long it will be before our laptops (laptops!) will be computing in teraflops, even petaflops, speeds now reached only in supercomputers (such as megahertz speeds once were).

Now consider getting from point A to point B; that is, travel? We can travel in just a few hours a distance that, for most of human history, could have taken weeks, even months.

Q&A FROM THE BIBLE

What is the fourth commandment?

"Remember the sabbath day, **to keep it holy**. Six days shalt thou labour, and do all thy work: but the seventh day is a sabbath unto the LORD thy God: in it thou shalt not do any work, thou, nor thy son, nor thy daughter, thy manservant, nor thy maidservant, nor thy cattle, nor thy stranger that is within thy gates" (Exodus 20:8-10).

Why is the Sabbath a special day?

"Hallow My Sabbaths, and they will be a **sign between Me and you**, that you may know that I am the LORD your God" (Ezekiel 20:20).

What are God's reasons for us to keep the Sabbath?

"For in six days **the LORD made the heavens and the earth**, the sea, and all that is in them, **and rested the seventh day**. Therefore the LORD blessed the Sabbath day and hallowed it" (Exodus 20:11).

"And **remember** that you were a slave in the land of Egypt, and the LORD your God **brought you out from there** by a mighty hand and by an outstretched arm; therefore the LORD your God commanded you to keep the Sabbath day" (Deuteronomy 5:15).

When do we see the first Sabbath kept in the Bible?

"Thus the heavens and the earth, and all the host of them, were finished. And on the seventh day God ended His work which He had done, and **He rested on the seventh day** from all His work which He had done. Then

WATCH visit **answrs.co/
sabbath** to watch a short video
about the Sabbath | 2:37

Harried, Harried, Harried

There's no doubt that we today can get things done at speeds that were unimaginable for most of human history.

And yet—what? With things getting done so much faster, the logical result would be that we should have so much more spare time to just chill out, right? Though that idea sure makes sense, it that how it really works?

Ask yourself this question: When was the last time you heard someone, or even yourself, say, "Wow, with my desktop CPU computing 1.5 billion computations per second, as opposed to only 1.5 million per second like my last one did, and my email getting to people in an instant compared to how long snail mail would take, or because I can travel from city to city or continent to continent in just a few hours, instead of days

God blessed the seventh day and sanctified it, because in it He rested from all His work which God had created and made" (Genesis 2:1-3).

Since the Sabbath was kept in the Garden of Eden who was it really intended for to keep and experience it?
"Then he said to them, 'The sabbath was **made for humankind**, and not humankind for the Sabbath'" (Mark 2:27, NRSV).

Did Jesus keep the Sabbath?
"So He came to Nazareth, where He had been brought up. And **as His custom was**, He **went into the synagogue** on the **Sabbath day**, and stood up to read" (Luke 4:16).

Did the apostles and Gentiles (non-Jews) keep the Sabbath after Jesus died and rose?
"So when the Jews went out of the synagogue, the **Gentiles** begged that these words might be preached **to them the next Sabbath**. On the next Sabbath almost the whole city came together to hear the word of God" (Acts 13:42, 44).

Which day is the Sabbath?
"but the **seventh day** is the Sabbath of the LORD your God" (Exodus 20:10).

Historically we know that Jesus rose on Sunday, so what is the seventh day Sabbath?
"Now **after the Sabbath**, as the **first day of the week began** to dawn, Mary Magdalene and the other Mary came to see the tomb. And behold, there was a great earthquake; for an angel of the Lord descended from heaven, and came and rolled back the stone from the door, and sat on it … But the angel answered and said to the women, 'Do not be afraid, for I know that you seek Jesus who was crucified. **He is not here; for He is risen**, as He said. Come, see the place where the Lord lay'" (Matthew 28:1-6).

or weeks—man, I have so much free time now to relax!"

It doesn't work that way, does it? On the contrary, no matter how much faster we get things done, we still never have enough time to rest, to relax, to chill. The faster we finish what we're doing, strangely enough, the less time we seem to have to relax. It's almost as certain and constant as the laws of physics. It could be called the Tyranny of Time Theory: The faster things get done, the more harried and rushed we become.

Enter the Sabbath

No wonder, then, that smack in the middle of the Ten Commandments, which is God's moral law, there is the commandment to rest. To chill out. To slow down. To stop working.

Right up there with the "thou shalt nots" about killing, stealing, idolatry and adultery—we find the commandment to rest on the Sabbath day. It's also the longest c o m m a n d m e n t among the ten, and it's pretty explicit:

"Remember the Sabbath day, to keep it holy. Six days you shall labor and do all your work, but the

WATCH

visit **answrs.co/day** to watch a video answering questions including *How can we know what day the Sabbath is?* and *Didn't Paul say that the law was nailed to the cross and abolished?*

seventh day is the Sabbath of the LORD your God. In it you shall do no work: you, nor your son, nor your daughter, nor your male servant, nor your female servant, nor your cattle, nor your stranger who is within your gates. For in six days the LORD made the heavens and the earth, the sea, and all that is in them, and rested the seventh day. Therefore the LORD blessed the Sabbath day and hallowed it" (Exodus 20:8-11).

The word "Sabbath" itself comes from a Hebrew root that means "to cease, to stop." That is, to cease hustling, to stop grabbing, grabbing, grabbing. To cease trying to get richer and richer, to stop trying to get more and more things. And if God knew that it was important for people 3000 years ago to stop, to rest, how much more important is it today?

One-Seventh of Our Lives

Notice, according to the commandment, we are to stop working on the seventh day. Why? Because God, our creator, created the world in six days, and He wanted us to remember the fact that, yes, He is the one who made all that was made (see John 1:3). In other words, we can get so caught up in

Q&A FROM THE BIBLE

When does the Sabbath begin?
"From **evening to evening**, you shall celebrate your sabbath" (Leviticus 23:32).

How do we keep the Sabbath holy?
"Six days shalt thou labour, and do all thy work: but the seventh day is a sabbath unto the LORD thy God: **in it thou shalt not do any work**, thou, nor thy son, nor thy daughter, thy manservant, nor thy maidservant, nor thy cattle, nor thy stranger that is within thy gates" (Exodus 20:9,10).

"**I warned them** about the day on which they were **selling provisions**. Men of Tyre dwelt there also, who brought in fish and all kinds of goods, and **sold them on the Sabbath** to the children of Judah, and in Jerusalem. Then I contended with the nobles of Judah, and said to them, 'What evil thing is this that you do, by which you **profane the Sabbath day**?'" (Nehemiah 13:15-17).

"If you turn away your foot from the Sabbath, **from doing your pleasure on My holy day**, and call the Sabbath a delight, the holy day of the LORD honorable, and shall honor Him, not doing your own ways, nor finding your own pleasure, nor speaking your own words" (Isaiah 58:13).

"And behold, there was a man who had a withered hand. And they asked Him, saying, 'Is it lawful to heal on the Sabbath?'–that they might accuse Him. Then He said to them, 'What man is there among you who has one sheep, and if it falls into a pit on the Sabbath, will not lay hold of it and lift it out? Of how much more value then is a man than a sheep? Therefore it is **lawful to do good** on the Sabbath'" (Matthew 12:10-12).

What special event should happen each Sabbath?
"There are six days when you may work, but the seventh day is a day of sabbath rest, **a day of sacred assembly**. You are not to do any work; wherever you live, it is a sabbath to the LORD" (Leviticus 23:3, NIV).

"And let us consider one another in order to stir up love and good works, **not forsaking the assembling of ourselves together**, as is the manner of some, but exhorting one another, and so much the more as you see the Day approaching" (Hebrews 10:24, 25).

"He came to Nazareth where he had been reared. As he always did on the Sabbath, he went to the **meeting place** [**synagogue** in other translations]" (Luke 4:16, The Message).

Does it really matter if I keep the Sabbath since it is just one of ten commandments?
"For whoever keeps the whole law but **fails in one point** has become **guilty of all of it**. For he who said, 'Do not commit adultery,' also said, 'Do not murder.' If you do not commit adultery but do murder, you have become a transgressor of the law" (James 2:10, 11, ESV).

What will eventually happen if I stop keeping God's commandments?
"Beware that you **do not forget the LORD** your God **by not keeping His commandments**, His judgments, and His statutes which I command you today" (Deuteronomy 8:11).

Will we keep the Sabbath in the New Earth?
"'For as the new heavens and the new earth which I will make shall remain before Me,' says the LORD, 'So shall your descendants and your name remain. And it shall come to pass that from one New Moon to another, and from **one Sabbath to another**, all flesh shall come to **worship before Me**,' says the LORD" (Isaiah 66:22, 23)

"*Seek* first the kingdom of God and His righteousness, and all these things shall be added to you."

Matthew 6:33

the day-to-day rat-race, swept up in the daily struggles and toils and intensity of just trying to survive and, then, THWACK!—God says, "Stop, chill, rest and remember that I am the One who created you and the world that you live in."

He doesn't recommend it, He doesn't suggest it—God commands it.

How fascinating, too, that God would directly link the seventh-day Sabbath to the creation event itself. The doctrine of creation, then, is so important that God demands one-seventh of our lives, every week and without exception, to remember it, something that He doesn't command for any other teaching. One-seventh of our lives to remember God as our creator and to recall that, far from being "blobs of organized mud" (see chapter two), we are beings created in the image of God, the One who put us here, and to whom we owe our existence and redemption.

The Lord of the Sabbath

All through the New Testament, when Jesus Christ was harangued by the religious leaders over the Sabbath, the issue was never which day to keep. Instead, the issue was how to rest on the seventh-day Sabbath, not whether one should or not, or whether one should rest on another day, such as Sunday. Thus, the "Sabbath controversies," as they are called by theologians, only affirm the continued validity of the seventh-day Sabbath rest. Nothing in these confrontations ever even hints that the Sabbath rest was to be done away with or that the true Sabbath was replaced by another day.

In fact, when attacked by the powers that be over what they perceived as a violation of the Sabbath, Jesus responded: "The Sabbath was made for man, and not man for the Sabbath. Therefore the Son of Man is also Lord of the Sabbath" (Mark 2:27, 28). Because the leaders had added a host of man-made rules that made the Sabbath a burden, Jesus sought to straighten them out by declaring that the Sabbath was "made for man." That is, the Sabbath day was created, all the way back in the Garden of Eden (see Genesis 2:1-3), to be a blessing to people— not a burden, which it became because of man-made made regulations that were not part of the original commandment.

The Divine Respite

On the contrary, the Sabbath was made to lessen burdens, especially the burden that comes from the clock. Not enough time. If only there were more time. Not enough hours in the day. Again, it comes down to The Tyranny of Time Theory: The faster things get done, the more harried and rushed we become.

The Sabbath, the fourth commandment, was "made for man," a divine respite from heaven to Earth, in which God has paved a way for us all, each week, to be freed from the continuous and unrelenting tyrant of time, which—even with our faster phones, faster cars, faster jets, faster internet connections—never lets us go.

MARK OF THE BEAST

15

Even the quickest reading of the Gospels shows the many times that Jesus was attacked by the powers that be over the Sabbath commandment. As the previous chapter showed, it wasn't over which day to keep but, instead, on how to keep it.

In one instance, Jesus approached a man with a withered hand and said to the leaders: "What man is there among you who has one sheep, and if it falls into a pit on the Sabbath, will not lay hold of it and lift it out? Of how much more value then is a man than a sheep? Therefore it is lawful to do good on the Sabbath" (Matthew 12:11). Jesus then healed the man, on the Sabbath day.

And how did the religious leaders respond? "But the Pharisees went out and plotted how they might kill Jesus" (Matthew 12:14, NIV). Kill Jesus? Over what? Over the seventh-day Sabbath?

This theme, that of the leaders persecuting, or even wanting to kill, Jesus over the seventh-day Sabbath echoes through the Gospels. We will come back to it shortly, too.

One-Seventh of Our Lives

As we also saw earlier, the doctrine of creation is so important, so foundational to faith, that not only was it memorialized in one of the Ten Commandments, but it is something that God demands one-seventh of our lives, one day every week, to remember—something that He asks with no other teaching. That fact alone shows just how important it must be.

From the first week in Eden, Sabbath has signified worship of the Creator, the true God. Indeed, worship has always been a crucial factor in the faith of God's people, and the book of Revelation teaches that, prior to Christ's Second Coming, worship will play a crucial role then, too. How so?

Worship the Beast and His Image

The book of Revelation is filled with symbols and images, many from the Old Testament, that recount the history of the church through the ages, as well as final events that lead to the Second Coming of Jesus and beyond.

According to Revelation, before Christ returns, a "beast" power, an apostate church-state regime (in Bible prophecy, animals symbolize political powers) will force the world to "worship the image of the beast" (Revelation 13:15). This means that people will be coerced into paying homage to this beast, an oppressive religious and political power.

The Commandments of the Creator

In contrast to those who worship the beast and his image, an angel from heaven calls for mankind to "worship Him who made heaven and earth, the sea and springs of water"—the Cre-

WATCH visit **answrs.co/themark** to watch a short video about the mark of the beast | 2:53

visit **answrs.co/beast** to watch *The Mark of the Beast* | 58:30

What immediately follows to completion of the work of the three angel's messages in Revelation 14:6-13?

"Then I looked, and behold, a white cloud, and **on the cloud sat One like the Son of Man**, having on His head a golden crown, and in His hand a sharp sickle. And another angel came out of the temple, crying with a loud voice to Him who sat on the cloud, 'Thrust in Your sickle and reap, for the time has come for You to reap, **for the harvest of the earth is ripe**.' So He who sat on the cloud thrust in His sickle on the earth, and **the earth was reaped**" (Revelation 14:14-16).

What does this harvest scene represent in Revelation?

"He answered and said unto them, He that soweth the good seed is the Son of man; the **field is the world**; the good seed are the children of the kingdom; but the tares are the children of the wicked one; the enemy that sowed them is the devil; the **harvest is the end of the world**; and the reapers are the angels" (Matthew 13:37-39).

Since the three angel's Messages are the last messages before the end of the world what do these messages warn us about?

"And the third angel followed them, saying with a loud voice, If any man **worship the beast** and his image, and **receive his mark in his forehead, or in his hand**, the same shall drink of the wine of the wrath of God, which is poured out without mixture into the cup of his indignation; and he shall be tormented with fire and brimstone in the presence of the holy angels, and in the presence of the Lamb" (Revelation 14:9,10).

Instead of receiving the mark of the beast, what does God want us to receive in our forehead?

"And I saw another angel ascending from the east, having the **seal of the living God**: and he cried with a loud voice to the four angels, to whom it was given to hurt the earth and the sea, saying, hurt not the earth, neither the sea, nor the trees. Till we have **sealed the servants of our God in their foreheads**" (Revelation 7:2,3).

Since the majority or Revelation is allusions and quotations from the Old Testament where in the Old Testament do we see God addressing putting something on our foreheads or hands?

"Now this is the **commandment**, and these are the statutes and judgments which the LORD your God has commanded to teach you, that you may observe them in the land which you are crossing over to possess ... and **these words which I command you** today **shall be** in your heart ... You shall **bind them** as a sign **on your hand**, and they shall be as **frontlets between your eyes**" (Deuteronomy 6:1,6-8).

Does God really want to seal us with His law?

"Bind up the testimony, **seal the law** among my disciples" (Isaiah 8:16).

Is this in harmony with God's new covenant for us today?

"Because finding fault with them, He says: "Behold, the days are coming, says the LORD, when I will make a **new covenant** with the house of Israel and with the house of Judah—not according to the covenant that I made with their fathers in the day when I took them by the hand to lead them out of the land of Egypt ... For this is the covenant that I will make with the house of Israel after those days, says the LORD: I will **put My laws in their mind** and write them on their hearts; and I will be their God, and they shall be My people" (Hebrews 8:8-10).

If the outward indicator is called a sign and the inner work is called a seal are both the outward sign and inner work essential for the Christian?
"And the LORD your God will **circumcise your heart** and the heart of your descendants, to **love the LORD your God** with all your heart and with all your soul, that you may live" (Deuteronomy 30:6).

What is another biblical word to describe the work of the Holy Spirit changing our hearts?
"Do you not know that the unrighteous will not inherit the kingdom of God? Do not be deceived. Neither fornicators, nor idolaters, nor adulterers, nor homosexuals, nor sodomites, nor thieves, nor covetous, nor drunkards, nor revilers, nor extortioners will inherit the kingdom of God. And such were some of you. But **you were washed**, but **you were sanctified**, but you were justified in the name of the Lord Jesus and **by the Spirit of our God**" (1 Corinthians 6:9-11).

Since the sealing work of God is Him sanctifying our minds and hearts what is the outward representation that this work is taking place?
"Moreover I also gave them My **Sabbaths**, to be **a sign** between them and Me, that they might know that I am the LORD **who sanctifies them**." (Ezekiel 20:12).

Since the Sabbath is the outward sign that God is writing His law in our minds and hearts then what is the real issue in the last days all about?
"Saying with a loud voice, 'Fear God and give glory to Him, for the hour of His judgment has come; and *worship* Him who made heaven and earth, the sea and springs of water'" (Revelation 14:7).

"Then a third angel followed them, saying with a loud voice, 'If anyone **worships the beast** and his image, and receives his mark on his forehead or on his hand'" (Revelation 14:9).

"And the smoke of their torment ascends forever and ever; and they have no rest day or night, who *worship* **the beast and his image**, and whoever receives the mark of his name" (Revelation 14:11).

See also Revelation 13:4, 8, 12, 15.

Since the seal of God has an outward expression of worship and the mark of the beast is Satan's counterfeit, would that make it also an expression of worship?
"He was granted power to give breath to the image of the beast, that the image of the beast should both speak and cause as many as would **not worship** the image of the beast to be killed. He causes all, both small and great, rich and poor, free and slave, **to receive a mark** on their right hand or on their foreheads" (Revelation 13:15,16).

What will the beast do to people in the last days?
"It also **forced all people** … to receive a mark on their right hands or on their foreheads" (Revelation 13:16, NIV).

But what will God's people choose in the last days?
"Here is the patience of the saints; here are those who keep the commandments of God and the faith of Jesus" (Revelation 14:12).

ator, the true God (Revelation 14:7). This angel's call actually reflects the language of the fourth commandment, the seventh-day Sabbath, which acknowledges Him who "made the heavens and the earth, the sea, and all that is in them," again the Creator, the true God (Exodus 20:11).

Thus, there's a direct link between the Sabbath commandment and the call to worship the Creator, in contrast to those who worship the beast and his image. Those who worship the Creator will manifest that worship by keeping His commandments, including the Sabbath commandment. The day that commandment refers to is the seventh-day Sabbath—Saturday, not Sunday, though Sunday is the day most commonly kept now among Christians, even though it is purely a man-made tradition that's not found the Bible, Old or New Testament.

In fact, history and Bible prophecy together show how a few centuries after the death of Jesus, the church, having drifted away from biblical truth, attempted to change the Sabbath to Sunday. This attempt was depicted in Scripture like this: "And [this power] shall intend to change times and law" (Daniel 7:25). This same power, which first attempted to change the Sabbath, reappears in the context of the mark of the beast and the end-time persecution. At this time, this power will "cause as many as would not worship the image of the beast to be killed" (Revelation 13:15).

In short, two classes of people will exist in the last days: 1) those who worship the beast and his image and 2) those who worship the true Creator. There doesn't seem to be any middle ground.

The Beast or the Creator?

Again, the issue in the final days is worship: Do we worship the beast and its image, or do we worship God, the Creator? Because those who worship the Creator are depicted as keeping the commandment of God, and because the seventh-day Sabbath is the only one of the "commandments of God" that specifically points to

the Lord as creator and to His creative power as the reason that He should be worshiped—many believe that the fourth commandment will play a vital role in this final conflict over worship at the end.

Death and persecution over the seventh-day Sabbath? Come on!

But have we not already seen this in the life of Jesus? In other words, this persecution would not be the first time something like this has happened, right?

Jesus Himself faced those who wanted Him killed over—yes—the seventh-day Sabbath. As we just saw, after He healed the man with the withered hand on the Sabbath, some people wanted Him dead. In another instance, when, on the Sabbath, Jesus healed a man who had been infirm for 38 years, how did the religious leaders act? The Bible says that they "persecuted Jesus, and sought to kill Him, because He had done these things on the Sabbath" (John 5:16).

Yes, it has happened before, to Jesus. Because God's faithful people not only keep the "commandments of God" but have "the faith of Jesus"; that is, they have faith like Jesus, which means they could experience what Jesus experienced. That's why, while most people will worship the beast and its image, similar persecution will happen to those who, like Jesus, keep the seventh-day Sabbath as the biblically mandated expression of their worship of the Creator instead of the beast.

NEWTON'S FORGOTTEN DISCOVERY

Giving Light to Our World

READ MORE + SHARE THIS TOPIC

Visit **www.glowonline.org/answer/newton** to read more about what you just read here. You can also share it on social media.

THE SECOND COMING

16

Though not so common anymore in the West, every now and then we hear of a kidnapping. The child of a wealthy family gets snatched, and the kidnappers demand ransom. Sometimes things turn out all right, in that the child is safely returned and the kidnappers are caught. Other times events don't conclude so happily.

One story, however, that we probably never heard: a child is kidnapped, and the parents pay a huge ransom. However, after paying the ransom—the parents never get the child!

Ridiculous, right? Well, this story can illustrate an important point about how ridiculous it would be if Jesus Christ did not return to the Earth.

What do we mean?

The Ransom

If it seemed implausible that the parents, after paying such an expensive ransom for their child, would not come to get that child, it's even more implausible that, having paid such an expensive ransom for us (His own life on the cross), Jesus Christ would not come get what He paid so dearly for. The Second Coming is, simply, Jesus Christ coming to retrieve what He paid a ransom for.

Look at the following texts:

"For there is one God and one mediator between God and men, the man Christ Jesus, who gave himself as a ransom for all men—the testimony given in its proper time" (1 Timothy 2:5, 6, NIV).

"For even the Son of Man came not to be served but to serve others and to give his life as a ransom for many" (Matthew 20:28, NLT).

The apostle Peter says that we were redeemed by "the precious blood of Christ" (1 Peter 1:19). The concept of "redeemed" reflects the concept of "ransomed." Christ paid for our redemption, our ransom, with His own life. And, in parallel with the story above—why would He have paid such a such a great price for us and yet not come back to get us?

The First Coming

One could argue, in fact, that the purpose of the first coming was the second. The first coming is what makes the second certain. If Jesus doesn't return, doesn't come back to get what He paid for with His own blood, then the first coming would have been a waste.

Let that thought sink in. Without the Second Coming, what Christ did at the first—from being born into humanity, to living a sinless life, to dying on the cross as the sacrifice for sin and being resurrected ... it all would have been for nothing. And who believes that?

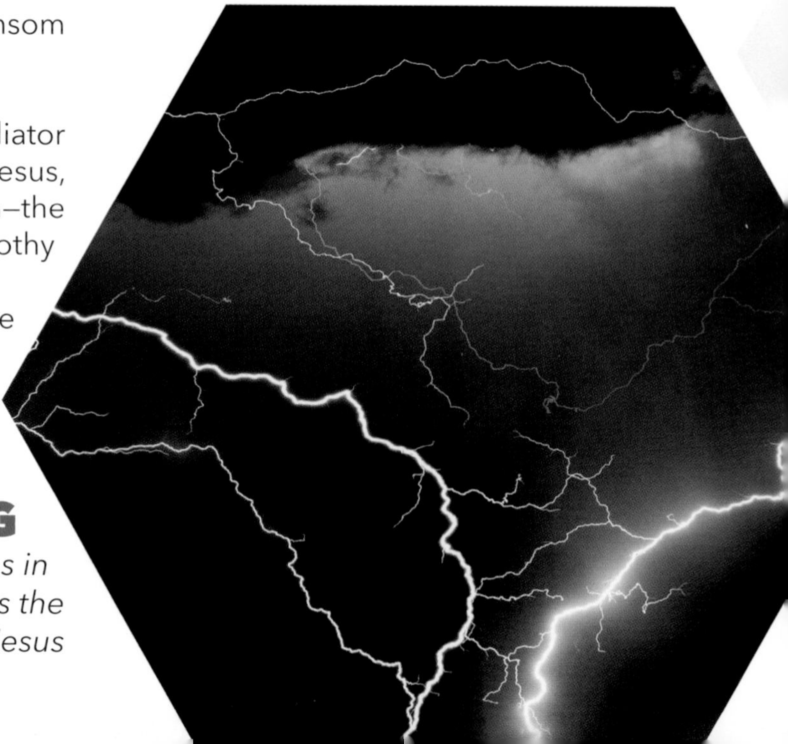

FACT ABOUT THE SECOND COMING

Approximately 1 out of every 25 verses in the New Testament refers to or mentions the Second Coming of Jesus

Left Behind?

For this reason (Jesus' death and promise of a return) and others, Christians since the early church have waited for and anticipated the return of Jesus. Thus, the question for most Christians isn't, "Will Jesus return?" but, rather, "How will He return?"

Years ago, books and movies came out called *Left Behind*, and they were about the Second Coming of Jesus. Unfortunately, the books and movies depicted the Second Coming as a secret event. True Christians were suddenly and secretly taken to heaven, with everyone else (the ones "left behind") wondering what happened to all those who had just vanished.

However popular that series was, the Scriptures present a radically different picture of Christ's return than what was depicted by the *Left Behind* saga.

Shout, Voice, and Trumpet

Read, for example, the following texts and, as you do, ask yourself what they teach about the manner of Christ's return:

"For the Lord himself will come down from heaven with a commanding shout, with the voice of the archangel, and with the trumpet call of God. First, the believers who have died will rise from their graves. Then, together with them, we who are still alive and remain on the earth will be caught up in the clouds to meet the Lord in the air. Then we will be with the Lord forever" (1 Thessalonians 4:16, 17, NLT).

"For as the lightning flashes in the east and shines to the west, so it will be when the Son of Man comes" (Mathew 24:27, NLT).

"Look! He comes with the clouds of heaven.

WATCH

visit **answrs.co/return** to watch a short video on the soon return of Jesus | 3:07

And everyone will see him" (Revelation 1:7, NLT).

"Behold, I tell you a mystery: We shall not all sleep, but we shall all be changed–in a moment, in the twinkling of an eye, at the last trumpet. For the trumpet will sound, and the dead will be raised incorruptible, and we shall be changed. For this corruptible must put on incorruption, and this mortal must put on immortality" (1 Corinthians 15: 52, 53).

"But the day of the Lord will come as a thief in the night, in which the heavens will pass away with a great noise, and the elements will melt with fervent heat; both the earth and the works that are in it will be burned up" (2 Peter 3:10, NKJV).

Christ's return will be like – what? Lightning across the sky. Every eye, that is every person, shall see Him. The dead in Christ shall be raised to life, which means that all of Christ's faithful followers through the ages, the millions who died and are under the dirt or their corpses dissolved in the sea, or wherever their remains are–they all will be brought back to life. Meanwhile, those who are alive when He comes will, in the twinkling of an eye, be physically transformed. Bodies of corruption and mortality will instantly be turned into bodies of incorruption and immortality. The Earth itself, with a "great noise," will melt and be burned, the precursor to a "new heaven and a new earth" (Revelation 21:1).

LISTEN IN visit **answrs.co/appearing** to listen to a presentation that goes along with what you're reading in this chapter.

The Return of Jesus

This powerful and glorious event is something nobody will miss

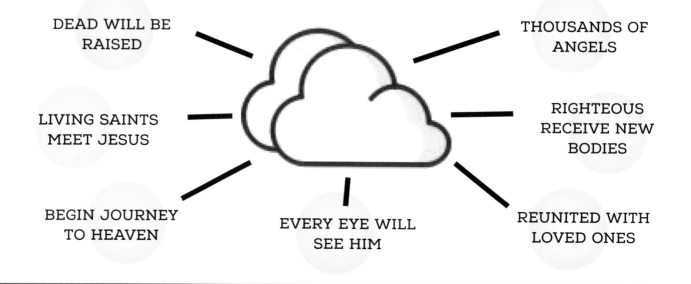

DEAD WILL BE RAISED

THOUSANDS OF ANGELS

LIVING SAINTS MEET JESUS

RIGHTEOUS RECEIVE NEW BODIES

BEGIN JOURNEY TO HEAVEN

EVERY EYE WILL SEE HIM

REUNITED WITH LOVED ONES

Q&A FROM THE BIBLE

Before Jesus went back to heaven, what promise did He make?
"In My Father's house are many mansions; if it were not so, I would have told you. I go to prepare a place for you. And if I go and prepare a place for you, **I will come again** and receive you to Myself; that where I am, there you may be also" (John 14:2, 3).

The disciples understood that Jesus' coming would mark what point in the world's history?
"Now as He sat on the Mount of Olives, the disciples came to Him privately, saying, 'Tell us, when will these things be? And what will be the sign of Your coming, and of the **end of the age**?'" (Matthew 24:3).

Why is it important for us to know what the Bible says about Jesus' Second Coming?
"Then if anyone says to you, 'Look, here is the Christ!' or 'There!' do not believe it. For false christs and false prophets will rise and show great signs and wonders to **deceive**, if possible, **even the elect**" (Matthew 24:24).

When Jesus went to Heaven what were the disciples told about how He would return?
"Who also said, 'Men of Galilee, why do you stand gazing up into heaven? This **same Jesus**, who was taken up from you into heaven, will so come **in like manner** as you saw Him go into heaven.'" (Acts 1:11).

What are the details about how Jesus went to Heaven?
"Now when He had spoken these things, while they watched, He was **taken up**, and a **cloud received Him** out of **their sight**. And while they **looked** steadfastly **toward heaven** as He **went up**, behold, two men stood by them in white apparel" (Acts 1:9,10).

Since they saw Jesus go up who will see Him when He returns?
"Behold, He is coming with clouds, and **every eye** will see Him, even they who pierced Him. And all the tribes of the earth will mourn because of Him. Even so, Amen" (Revelation 1:7).

The Secret Rapture?

With all due respect, the Bible does not support the popularized view in the *Left Behind* series about the Second Coming of Jesus, including what has been called "the secret rapture." The "rapture" part, which means that the those who are alive when Jesus returns will be taken immediately up to heaven—yes, that's true. After all, we just read that "we who are still alive and remain on the earth will be caught up in the clouds to meet the Lord in the air. Then we will be with the Lord forever."

But, as we just read as well, when this rapture happens, it will be announced by "a commanding shout, with the voice of the archangel, and with the trumpet." A commanding shout? The voice of an angel? The trumpet of God? Whatever else Scripture teaches about the Second Coming, it's

WATCH

visit **answrs.co/secondcoming** to watch
The Second Coming of Jesus | 58:30

not going to be a quiet and secret event.

And, certainly, not a silent one!

The idea of faithful Christians just standing there in a crowd, or sitting next to you on an

---

"For as the **lightning** comes **from the east** and **flashes to the west**, so also will the coming of the Son of Man be" (Matthew 24:27).

Who will be with Jesus when He returns?
"When the Son of Man comes in His glory, and **all the holy angels** with Him, then He will sit on the throne of His glory." (Matthew 25:31).

What happens first when Jesus returns?
"For the Lord Himself shall descend from heaven with a shout, with the voice of the archangel, and with the trump of God: and the **dead in Christ shall rise first**" (1 Thessalonians 4:16, KJV).

What will happen to faithful Christians after the dead in Christ rise?
"Then we that are **alive**, that are left, shall together with them **be caught up** in the clouds, to **meet the Lord** in the air: and so shall we ever be with the Lord" (1 Thessalonians 4:17, ASV).

Where will we finally meet the Lord?
"Then we that are alive, that are left, shall together with them be caught up **in the clouds**, to meet the Lord **in the air**: and so shall we

ever be with the Lord" (1 Thessalonians 4:17, ASV).

What will we be like when we are caught up to meet the Lord in the air?
"Behold, I tell you a mystery: We shall not all sleep, but **we shall all be changed**—in a moment, in the twinkling of an eye, at the last trumpet. For the trumpet will sound, and the dead will be raised incorruptible, and we shall be changed. For this **corruptible** must put on **incorruption**, and this **mortal** must put on **immortality**. So when this corruptible has put on incorruption, and this mortal has put on immortality, then shall be brought to pass the saying that is written: 'Death is swallowed up in victory'" (1 Corinthians 15:51-54).

What response did Jesus say we should have it anyone says He came secretly?
"Wherefore if they shall say unto you, Behold, he is in the desert; go not forth: behold, he is in the **secret** chambers; **believe it not**" (Matthew 24:26, KJV).

What will the righteous say when Jesus returns?
"And it will be said in that day: 'Behold, this is

Q&A FROM THE BIBLE

our God; We have **waited for Him**, and **He will save us**. This is the LORD; we have waited for Him; we will **be glad and rejoice** in His salvation" (Isaiah 25:9).

What will the wicked respond when Jesus returns?

"And then shall appear the sign of the Son of man in heaven: and then shall all the tribes of the earth **mourn**, and they shall see the Son of man coming in the clouds of heaven with power and great glory" (Matthew 24:30).

"And said to the mountains and rocks, '**Fall on us and hide us** from the face of Him who sits on the throne and from the wrath of the Lamb! For the great day of His wrath has come, and who is able to stand?'" (Revelation 6:16,17).

What are we to do today so that we can be part of that group Jesus is coming back to take home?

"And now, little children, **abide in Him**, that when He appears, we may have confidence and not be ashamed before Him at His coming" (1 John 2:28).

What should every person do that has this hope that Jesus will return?

"And everyone who has this hope in Him **purifies himself**, just as He is pure" (1 John 3:3).

What should we say to one another since we have this hope of the Second Coming?

"Say to them that are of a fearful heart, **Be strong, fear not**: behold, **your God will come** … he will come **and save you**" (Isaiah 35:4).

Q&A: The Second Coming

WATCH visit answrs.co/taken

to watch a video answering questions including *What does it mean when it says "One will be taken and one will be left? Which group will be taken and which will be left?"* What does the Bible mean when it says *"Until the day of Jesus Christ in Philippians 1:6?"* and *When the Bible says that Jesus will come as a theif in the night, doesn't that mean it will be secret?*

airplane or driving next to you in a car, and then just quietly disappearing, with nothing remaining of them but their clothes, is more science fiction that biblical truth. This idea might make good material for Hollywood, but it has no foundation in Scripture.

The Certainty of the Second Coming

One day, like lightning, with the trumpet sound of God, Jesus Christ will return. No more would parents who paid a ransom for their child not come back to get that child, than would Jesus, having paid the ransom for us, not come back to take us home.

That's the certainty we can have of the Second Coming of Jesus, like lightning across the sky, coming back for us.

READ MORE + SHARE THIS TOPIC

Visit **www.glowonline.org/answer/hope** to read more about what you just read here. You can also share it on social media.

17

THE MILLENNIUM

A Thousand Years of Answers

Sin and evil have undoubtedly touched this planet. In fact, Scripture says the "whole creation groans and labors" under it (Romans 8:22). Yet however much sin and evil have defaced the Earth, evidence not only of God's existence—but also of His love—abounds in the cosmos.

But, still ... the suffering. Many thoughtful people, open to the idea of God, struggle with the reality of suffering in a world created by God. And though *The Answer Book*, in chapter 9, dealt with the challenge of suffering, many of us still have questions.

Well, the good news is that, before sin, evil and all their wretched consequences are eradicated forever, God will give His people a special time, a thousand years, actually, during which their deepest questions will be answered.

This time is called the millennium. What is the millennium, where will it be, and what will happen during its thousand years?

The Second Coming

As we saw in the last chapter, when Jesus returns to the Earth, the dead in Christ will be resurrected—and they, with the living faithful, will be "caught up in the clouds to meet the Lord in the air. Then we will be with the Lord forever" (1 Thessalonians 4:16, 17). The event fulfills the words of Jesus when He said: "I will come again and receive you to Myself; that where I am, there you may be also" (John 14:3).

While the Second Coming is good news for God's faithful, for the lost it's, unfortunately, not so good. Like the people during the Flood who didn't get on Noah's ark before the water came (Matthew 24:37-39) or those in Sodom and Gomorrah who didn't leave before the fire (Luke 17:28-30)—they will face death. As the prophet Isaiah described it: "For behold, the LORD comes out of His place to punish the inhabitants of the earth for their iniquity; the earth will also disclose her blood, and will no more cover her slain" (Isaiah 26:21).

A Desolate Earth

So, after Christ returns, the saved are with Him in heaven, the lost are slain, and the Earth becomes desolate and empty. "I beheld the earth, and indeed it was without form, and void. I beheld, and indeed there was no man" (Jeremiah 4:23, 25). The words, "without form and void," point directly back to the Earth's desolate state at the beginning of creation, depicted as "without form and void" (Genesis 1:2). It's as if the original creation were undone.

During this time, Scripture says that Satan will be "bound ... for a thousand

1ST RESURRECTION & SECOND COMING — 2ND RESURRECTION & HOLY CITY DESCENDS

1,000 YEARS

WATCH visit **answrs.co/millennium** to watch a short video about the thousand years | 2:04

visit **answrs.co/lake** to watch *Revelation's Lake of Fire* | 58:31

What event comes before the 1,000 year event known as the millennium?

"For **the Lord himself shall descend from heaven**, with a shout, with the voice of the archangel, and with the trump of God: and the dead in Christ shall rise first" (1 Thessalonians 4:16, KJV).

What happens to the wicked at this event?

"And the **rest were killed with the sword** which proceeded from the mouth of Him who sat on the horse. And all the **birds were filled** with their flesh" (Revelation 19:21).

What happens to Satan at this event?

"Then I saw an angel coming down from heaven, having the key to the bottomless pit and a great chain in his hand. He laid hold of the dragon, that serpent of old, who is the Devil and Satan, and **bound him for a thousand years**; and he cast him **into the bottomless pit**, and shut him up, and set a seal on him, so that he should deceive the nations no more till the thousand years were finished. But after these things he must be released for a little while" (Revelation 20:1-3).

What is the condition of the planet during this 1000 years?

"I **beheld the earth**, and indeed it was **without form, and void**; and the heavens, they **had no light**. I beheld the mountains, and indeed they trembled, and all the hills moved back and forth. I beheld, and indeed **there was no man**, and all the birds of the heavens had fled. I beheld, and indeed **the fruitful land was a wilderness**, and **all its cities were broken down at the presence of the LORD**, by His fierce anger. For thus says the LORD: 'The whole land shall be desolate; yet I will not make a full end'" (Jeremiah 4:23-27).

This event is the return of Jesus at His second coming, so what will happen to the righteous at when it takes place?

"The Lord Himself will descend from heaven with a shout, with the voice of an archangel, and with the trumpet of God. And the **dead in Christ will rise first**. Then we who are **alive and remain shall be caught up together with them** in the clouds to meet the Lord in years" (Revelation 20:2) in a "bottomless pit" and will remain there "so that he should deceive the nations no more till the thousand years were finished" (Revelation 20:3). The Greek for "bottomless pit" (*abussos*, from which we get the word "abyss") also reflects what the Earth was like when it was "without form and void."

A Thousand Years in Heaven

While Satan is chained to a desolate and depopulated Earth, God's redeemed are in heaven where they, actually, are involved with judging, not just the world, but angels as well. "Do you not know that the saints will judge the world? Do you not know that we shall judge angels?" (1 Corinthians 6:2, 3). Revelation depicts the period like this: "And I saw thrones, and they sat on them, and judgment was committed to them. ... And they lived and reigned with Christ for a thousand years" (Revelation 20:4). It also says: "Blessed and holy is he who has part in the first resurrection. Over such the second death has no power, but they shall be priests of God and of Christ, and shall reign with Him a thousand years" (Revelation 20:6).

Imagine being in heaven and knowing that a loved one was lost whom you expected to be there. You may experience pain and wonder why. How nice to get to know all the facts, all the evidence, and to know for yourself the goodness and justice of God amid all the evil and suffering. This is why the redeemed in heaven will one day shout: "Even so, Lord God Almighty, true and righteous are Your judgments" (Revelation 16:7). Here, where many of the questions about suffering, evil, and pain will be raised, they will be answered, too.

the air. And thus we shall always be with the Lord" (1 Thessalonians 4:16).

How many resurrections will there be?
"Do not marvel at this; for the hour is coming in which all who are in the graves will hear His voice and come forth—those who have done good, to the **resurrection of life**, and those who have done evil, to the **resurrection of condemnation**" (John 5:28, 29).

"…This is **the first resurrection**. Blessed and holy is he who has part in **the first resurrection**" (Revelation 20:5,6).

The righteous living and dead go up to be with the Lord at the Second Coming, but what will they do with Him?
"And I saw thrones, and they sat on them, and **judgment was committed to them**. Then I saw the souls of those who had been beheaded for their witness to Jesus and for the word of God…and they **lived and reigned** with Christ for a **thousand years**" (Revelation 20:4,5).

Will we really have a role to participate in God's judgment?

"Do you not know that **we shall judge angels**? How much more, things that pertain to this life?" (1 Corinthians 6:3).

What and who are we really judging in the judgment?
"And now, O inhabitants of Jerusalem and men of Judah, **judge**, please, **between Me and My vineyard**. What **more could have been done** to My vineyard **that I have not done** in it? … For the vineyard of the LORD of hosts is the house of Israel" (Isaiah 5:3, 4, 7).

When we sit in judgment and see that God did all that He could have done to save those who are not in heaven what will the righteous in heaven say?
"They sing the song of Moses, the servant of God, and the song of the Lamb, saying: "Great and marvelous are Your works, Lord God Almighty! **Just and true are Your ways**, O King of the saints!" (Revelation 15:3).

What takes place at the end of the 1000 year millennium?
"But the **rest of the dead** did not live again until the thousand years were finished" (Revelation 20:5).

The Second Resurrection

After the thousand years end, what happens? "But the rest of the dead did not live again until the thousand years were finished" (Revelation 20:5). Scripture talks of two resurrections, "those who have done good, to the resurrection of life, and those who have done evil, to the resurrection of condemnation" (John 5:29). Because the resurrection of life, for those who have "done good," happened at the Second Coming, Revelation 20:5 is the resurrection of those who have "done evil." Hence, the dead coming back to life after the thousand years is the resurrection of condemnation.

Notice, too, Scripture says that at the end of the thousand years not only will the dead rise but that "when the thousand years have expired, Satan will be released from his prison" (Revelation 20:7). This means that Satan is not trapped on Earth alone anymore; he now has the resurrected dead to continue to deceive.

In fact, Revelation depicts what happens next: Satan "will go out to deceive the nations which are in the four corners of the earth, Gog and Magog, to gather them together to battle, whose number is as the sand of the sea. They went up on the breadth of the earth and surrounded the camp of the saints and the beloved city. And fire came down from God out of heaven and devoured them" (Revelation 20:8, 9).

The Real Hell

In short, the lost dead, now resurrected, but still in rebellion against God, seek to attack the Holy City of God, the "New Jerusalem, coming down out of heaven from God, prepared as a bride adorned for her husband" (Revelation 21:2). However, as the text above says, fire from

God came down and "devoured them."

Devoured, as in destroyed, as in consumed, as in "everlasting destruction" (2 Thessalonians 1:9). We saw in chapter 13 that this is the ultimate and final fate of the lost. That is, it's these people going back to the nothingness out of which they came. This is what Scripture refers to, numerous times, as "the second death" (Revelation 2:11; 20:6, 14; 21:8), in which the lost receive what Scripture says is their "just reward" (Hebrews 2:2). And it's hard to imagine even the worst sinner's "just reward" as billions and billions and billions of eons being consciously tormented in an eternally burning fire.

That's not what a just God would do.

The Justice of God

What a just God does is, instead, revealed in the millennium. Notice that this final punishment of the lost does not occur until after the millennium, until after "judgment was committed to them," that is, to the saints in heaven. Before the lost face final punishment, the saved will see for themselves how just and fair and loving God is in dealing with the lost; indeed, the saved will have

WATCH visit **answrs.co/converted** to watch a video answering questions including *Will everyone be converted during the millennium?* and *What will Satan be doing on earth during the millennium if all the people here are dead?*

a role in the judgment of the lost. The process will be so fair that the redeemed will shout: "Even so, Lord God Almighty, true and righteous are Your judgments" (Revelation 16:7).

Hence, the teaching of the millennium, where the difficult question of suffering and evil will, yes, also be brought to the best resolution possible.

Q&A FROM THE BIBLE

What else will happen at the end of the thousand years besides the resurrection of the wicked?
"Now when the thousand years have expired, **Satan will be released from his prison** and will go out to deceive the nations which are in the four corners of the earth, Gog and Magog, to gather them together to battle, whose number is as the sand of the sea" (Revelation 20:7, 8).

What happens to the wicked when they try to take the city of God by force?
"They went up on the breadth of the earth and surrounded the camp of the saints and the beloved city. And **fire came down from God out of heaven and devoured them**" (Revelation 20:9).

Did God desire for any humans to experience this final destruction called the second death?
"'As I live,' says the Lord GOD, 'I have **no pleasure in the death of the wicked**, but that the wicked turn from his way and live. Turn, turn from your evil ways! For why should you die, O house of Israel?'" (Ezekiel 33:11).

"Then He will also say to those on the left hand, 'Depart from Me, you cursed, into the everlasting fire **prepared for the devil and his angels**'" (Matthew 25:41).

What event follows the destruction of the wicked on earth?
"Now I saw a **new heaven and a new earth**, for the first heaven and the first earth had passed away" (Revelation 21:2).

18

HEAVEN

A Heavenly Earth

A T-shirt reads: "It's not that life is so short, but that death is so long. ... John 3:16."

Good point, actually. No matter how long we live—20 years, 94 years—one thing is indisputable: Whatever comes after we die will last a lot longer than how long we lived. Infinitely longer.

It would seem, therefore, that the most logical pursuit any human could take would be: 1) Find out what comes after death, and 2) make any choices that could determine, if possible, what their fate would be after they die. Because, again, whatever comes after death will be a lot longer than what came before.

Eternal Life

The good news is that God loves us and that, because of Christ' death, we can have eternal life.

"For God so loved the world that He gave His only begotten Son, that whoever believes in Him should not perish but have everlasting life" (John 3:16).

"However, for this reason I obtained mercy, that in me first Jesus Christ might show all longsuffering, as a pattern to those who are going to believe on Him for everlasting life" (1 Timothy 1:16).

"Whoever eats My flesh and drinks My blood has eternal life, and I will raise him up at the last day" (John 6:54).

"He who loves his life will lose it, and he who hates his life in this world will keep it for eternal life" (John 12:25).

The Word of God is clear: Through Jesus, through faith in what He did for us on the cross, we can have eternal life.

The choice we have, then, is to accept that life.

Who Would Want to Live Forever?

A woman facing death said to her accuser, "I have the promise of eternal life."

To which her accuser responded, "Who in their right mind would want eternal life?"

Considering how hard our existence can be here, who would want to live forever? Fair question. But when the Bible talks about "eternal life," it's not talking about life as fallen beings in a fallen world. On the contrary, it's referring to a whole new existence for us, in new bodies, in a new heaven and

I go to prepare a place for you. And if I go and prepare a place for you, I will come again and receive you to Myself; that where I am, there you may be also.

WATCH

visit **answrs.co/heaven** to see a short video about heaven

2:55

WATCH

visit **answrs.co/what** to watch a video answering questions including *What will we do in heaven?*, *Where is heaven located?* and *If we get new bodies in heaven, how will we know each other?*

new earth. "'For as the new heavens and the new earth which I will make shall remain before Me,' says the LORD, "So shall your descendants and your name remain'" (Isaiah 66:22).

"Remain" ... as in forever.

A Purging Fire

As we have seen in *The Answer Book*, the faithful dead sleep in the grave (see chapter 11) until the Second Coming of Jesus, when they are resurrected to life, eternal life, in new bodies (see chapter 16). After 1000 years in heaven, the millennium, where they will reign as judges, the Holy City, Jerusalem, comes down from heaven to the Earth—"the New Jerusalem, coming down out of heaven from God, prepared as a bride adorned for her husband" (Revelation 21:2)—and the lost are resurrected from death to face just punishment for their sins (see chapter 17).

At this point, the fire that ultimately destroys the lost—forever—is the fire that burns up this old Earth, ultimately cleansing and purging it from all the devastation caused by sin.

LISTEN IN

visit **answrs.co/home** to listen to a presentation that goes along with what you're reading in this chapter.

"But the day of the Lord will come as a thief in the night, in which the heavens will pass away with a great noise, and the elements will melt with fervent heat; both the earth and the works that are in it will be burned up. ... Nevertheless we, according to His promise, look for new heavens and a new earth in which righteousness dwells" (2 Peter 3:10, 13).

A New Heaven and Earth

A new heavens and a new Earth (in this context, the word "heavens" means the sky above the Earth). Here is where it all ends—or should we say, "Here is where it all begins again"? Under this new heaven, and on this new Earth, the redeemed live forever, enjoying the eternal life given them in Jesus.

All we have known, or ever known, is sin and death. But, as we saw in chapter 8 on "The Great Controversy," this was never supposed to have happened. It is an aberration. But, even before the creation, God knew what was going to happen, and thus, Jesus, "the Lamb slain from the foundation of the world" (Revelation 13:8), had already determined to come to this world, to live a perfect life in our behalf, and then die for us—giving every human being the chance to have the eternal life that God wanted us to have to begin with.

The Place Prepared for Us

Jesus said, "In My Father's house are many

Q&A FROM THE BIBLE

Why did God originally create the earth?
"For thus says the LORD, who created the heavens, who is God, who formed the earth and made it, who has established it, who did not create it in vain, who **formed it to be inhabited**" (Isaiah 45:18).

How was our Earth originally created?
"Then God saw everything that He had made, and indeed it was **very good**. So the evening and the morning were the sixth day" (Genesis 1:31).

What happened to the planet itself when Adam and Eve sinned?
"Then to Adam He said, 'Because you have heeded the voice of your wife, and have eaten from the tree of which I commanded you, saying, 'You shall not eat of it.' **Cursed is the ground** for your sake; In toil you shall eat of it all the days of your life" (Genesis 3:17).

"For the **creation waits** in eager expectation for the children of God to be revealed. For **the creation was subjected to frustration**, not by its own choice, but by the will of the one who subjected it, in hope that **the creation itself** will be **liberated** from its **bondage to decay** and brought into the freedom and glory of the children of God. We know that the whole **creation has been groaning** as in the pains of childbirth right up to the present time (Romans 8:19-22, NIV).

Since the Earth itself is effected by the curse of sin is it, as it is today, our true home?
"These all died in faith, not having received the promises, but having seen them afar off were assured of them, embraced them and confessed that they were **strangers and pilgrims on the earth**. For those who say such things declare plainly that they **seek a** homeland…But now they desire **a better**, that is, a **heavenly country**" (Hebrews 11:13-16).

What has God prepared for each of us?
"But now they desire a better, that is, a heavenly country. Therefore God is not ashamed to be called their God, for He has **prepared a city** for them" (Hebrews 11:16).

"In My Father's house are **many mansions**; if it were not so, I would have told you. I go to **prepare a place for you**. And if I go and prepare a place for you, I will come again and receive you to Myself; that where I am, there you may be also" (John 14:2,3).

Where is the Father's house where Jesus is preparing a place for us?
"Unto You I lift up my eyes, O You who **dwell in the heavens**" (Psalm 123:1).

What is the name of this city in Heaven which God has prepared for us?
"Then I, John, saw the **holy city, New Jerusalem**, coming down out of heaven from God, prepared as a bride adorned for her husband" (Revelation 21:2).

What is in the middle of this city?
"And he showed me a pure river of **water of life**, clear as crystal, proceeding from the throne of God and of the Lamb. In the middle of its street, and on either side of the river, was the **tree of life**, which bore twelve fruits, each tree yielding its fruit every month. The leaves of the tree were for the healing of the nations" (Revelation 22:1, 2).

What is significant about eating fruit from the tree of life?
"Take also of the tree of life, and **eat**, and **live forever**" (Genesis 3:22).

Will this city stay in Heaven forever?
"Then I, John, saw the holy city, New Jerusalem, **coming down out of heaven** from God, prepared as a bride adorned for her husband" (Revelation 21:2).

"Blessed are the meek, for they shall **inherit the earth**" (Matthew 5:5).

Since the earth itself is cursed with sin what will God do so our heavenly city can be here?
"For behold, I create **new heavens** and a **new earth**; and the former shall not be remembered or come to mind" (Isaiah 65:17).

What will happen to this "old" world?
"But the day of the Lord will come as a thief in the night, in which the heavens will pass away with a great noise, and **the elements will melt with fervent heat**; both the earth and the works that are in it will be burned up" (2 Peter 3:10).

Who will be able to be a part of the New Jerusalem in the New Earth?
"Blessed are those who **do His commandments**, that they may have the **right to the tree of life**, and **may enter** through the gates into the city" (Revelation 22:14).

"Blessed be the God and Father of our Lord Jesus Christ, who according to His **abundant mercy** has begotten us again to **a living hope through the resurrection of Jesus Christ** from the dead, to an **inheritance incorruptible** and undefiled and that does not fade away, reserved in heaven for you" (1 Peter 1:3,4).

"For God so loved the world that He gave His only begotten Son, that whoever **believes in Him** should not perish but have **everlasting life**" (John 3:16).

What will the new earth be like?
"And God will **wipe away every tear** from their eyes; there shall be **no more death, nor sorrow, nor crying**. There shall be **no more pain**, for the **former things have passed away**. Then He who sat on the throne said, 'Behold, I make all things new.' And He said to me, 'Write, for these words are true and faithful'" (Revelation 21:4,5).

"The **wolf** also **shall dwell with the lamb**, the leopard shall lie down with the young goat, the calf and the young lion and the fatling together; and a little child shall lead them. And the **lion shall eat straw like the ox**. The nursing child shall play by the cobra's hole, and the weaned child shall put his hand in the viper's den. They shall **not hurt nor destroy** in all My holy mountain" (Isaiah 11:6-9).

"And I heard a loud voice from heaven saying, 'Behold, the tabernacle of God is with men, and He will dwell with them, and they shall be His people. **God Himself will be with them and be their God**'" (Revelation 21:3).

mansions; if it were not so, I would have told you. I go to prepare a place for you. And if I go and prepare a place for you, I will come again and receive you to Myself; that where I am, there you may be also" (John 14:2, 3). The new heaven, the new Earth—this is where He will be and where we will be with Him, too. A place without sin, war, crime, and death, but with Jesus, here, among us—a heavenly Earth. That's what Jesus went to the cross for, so that each one of us could be there with Him—again, in a world without all the things that make life so miserable here.

Only one reminder of what went on before will remain: Jesus will ever bear the marks of His crucifixion. Upon His wounded head, His side, His hands and feet will be the only traces of what sin has wrought. Christ, the only sinless One, will forever carry the scars of sin so that we, having once been sinners, will never have to.

Yes, death, for now, for the living, seems long. But it's nothing compared to eternal life in the heavenly new Earth, which awaits all who claim, by faith, what Jesus Christ has done.

The eternal awaits us. Eternal life or eternal destruction.

Your call.

19

GOD'S PEOPLE

Organized Religion

In recent years, a new word has appeared for what's not a new phenomenon. The word is "nones"; it refers to the millions of Americans who don't affiliate with any religion or religious belief. The reasons vary: nones are agnostic, atheist, distrustful of doctrine, or disdainful of religious leaders or their social stands.

Another reason, one that that echoes across the years, is that the nones don't like "organized religion."

What, then, would they prefer—"disorganized religion" instead?

The *Qahal*

There's no question that so-called "organized religion" hasn't always been a paradigm of sweetness and light, to say the least. A Marxist literary critic (a Marxist!), Terry Eagleton, and no friend of the faith, wrote the following: "There is a document that records God's endless, dispiriting struggle with organized religion, known as the Bible."

A clever line, actually. And true to a great degree. Starting with the Bible's first "organized" religion, called the *qahal*, the "congregation," which was the Hebrews on their way out of Egypt, the Bible does depict what could be called "God's endless, dispiriting struggle with organized religion."

Nevertheless, a key teaching of the Bible is that God does have a group of people who band together to help each other and to minister to the needs of our hurting world. However bad a rap it has gotten, and not always unjustifiably so,

"organized religion" is part and parcel of biblical faith.

This organized religion is known, today, as the "church." What is the idea of the "church," and why should anyone who loves Jesus join one?

It's to these questions that we turn.

The Called-Out Ones

The New Testament teaches about the importance of the church, which is from the Greek word *ekklesia*, "a calling out," the idea of people called out of the world, called out of their old life, and called into a new life where they can help each other and preach the gospel.

The Lord had originally called out the Hebrew nation. It was to be an organized unity that would spread the knowledge of the true God to a world steeped in paganism, child sacrifice, polytheism, and idolatry. After the death and resurrection of Jesus, the Christian church—made of Jews and Gentiles, anyone who believed in Jesus—took on that role.

The Images of the Church

The New Testament uses numerous images to describe the church. For instance, the church is depicted as a body (Ephesians 2:16; 1 Corinthians 12:13; Ephesians 5:23). The idea is that just as hands, or eyes,

WATCH

visit **answrs.co/church** to see a short video about God's people | 2:28

or feet, or stomach cannot function optimally without each other, the church, as a body, needs different people with different gifts to keep it functioning properly.

The New Testament also talks about the church as a "temple," even as "the temple of God" (1 Corinthians 3:16). In other words, the church should be a sacred place where people's lives and characters and selflessness reveal to the world the love and character of the God whom they serve. Jesus Himself talked about this idea when He said that His church is "the light of the world," a city set on a hill that "cannot be hidden" and "the salt of the earth" (Matthew 5:13-15). The Bible also talks about the church as a "bride," the idea centering around a key Christian teaching: God's love for His people and His people's love for Him. This concept, though first appearing in the Old Testament—"I will betroth you to Me forever; Yes, I will betroth you to Me in righteousness and justice, In lovingkindness and mercy" (Hosea 2:19), reappears in the New, too. Here, Paul writes about the church: "For I have betrothed you to one husband, that I may present you as a chaste virgin to Christ" (2 Corinthians 11:2).

The Fellowship

Another key point about the church is of "fellowship," of a close relationship with fellow believers. "But if we walk in the light as He is in the light, we have fellowship with one another, and the blood of Jesus Christ His Son cleanses us from all sin" (1 John 1:7). Being part of a church makes you part of a something so much greater than yourself, a body that can help you

Q&A: God's People

WATCH

visit **answrs.co/member** to watch a video answering questions including *Do I have to be a member of a church to be saved?*, and *Why would I want to join a church when there's so many hypocrites there?*

in times of need and that enables you to help others in their time of need.

However much most people want to be independent, to be on their own (we live in a culture of what has been called "rugged individualism"), the fact is that, at times, we need others. Sometimes we just can't make it on our own. More importantly, others, at times, need us—and the church, an "organized religion," provides a powerful and effective means of making available that needed help.

Which Church?

Of course, all this leads to a rational and logical question: Which church should someone who believes in Jesus join? After all, there are so many out there, thousands of different denominations. So how does one go about choosing a church, particularly the right one?

First of all, God has faithful people everywhere. Salvation is not found through church membership; salvation is found only through a personal acceptance of Christ's righteousness, which is offered to us by faith. "These things have I written unto you that believe on the name of the Son of God; that ye may know that ye have eternal life, and that ye may believe on the name of the Son of God" (1 John 5:13, KJV).

Nevertheless, the Lord has, in His Word, given us clear depictions of what His end-time church will look like. What follows is a summary of the

Q&A FROM THE BIBLE

What were God's people in the wilderness called?
"This is he, that was in **the church** in the wilderness with the angel which spake to him in the mount Sina, and with our fathers: who received the lively oracles to give unto us" (Acts 7:38, KJV).

Who are the people that compose the church?
"Praising God and having favor with all the people. And the Lord added to the church daily **those who were being saved**" (Acts 2:47).

"Then those who gladly **received his word were baptized**; and that day about three thousand souls were **added to them**" (Acts 2:41).

What is the church considered?
"I write so that you may know how you ought to conduct yourself in **the house of God, which is the church** of the living God, the pillar and ground of the truth" (1 Timothy 3:15).

What should the church be?
"Which is the church of the living God, **the pillar and ground of the truth**" (1 Timothy 3:15).

What is the source of truth?
"Sanctify them by Your truth. **Your word is truth**" (John 17:17).

What should the church do with the truth?
"So it was that for a whole year they assembled with the church and **taught a great many people**. And the disciples were first called Christians in Antioch" (Acts 11:26).

"**Preach the word!** Be ready in season and out of season. Convince, rebuke, exhort, **with all** longsuffering and **teaching**" (2 Timothy 4:2).

What did Jesus teach should be at the center of what we teach from the Bible?
"You search the Scriptures, for in them you think you have eternal life; and these are they which **testify of Me**" (John 5:39).

What does the Bible say people will want from the church as we near the end?
"For the time will come when they will **not endure sound doctrine**, but according to their **own desires**, because they have itching ears, they will **heap up for themselves teachers**" (2 Timothy 4:3).

What should God's ministers be doing to the church?
"And he went through Syria and Cilicia, **strengthening the churches**" (Acts 15:41).

What are some of the gifts God has given to His church?
"And He Himself gave some to be **apostles**, some **prophets**, some **evangelists**, and some **pastors** and **teachers**" (Ephesians 4:11).

Why were these gifts given to the church?
"For the **equipping of the saints** for the **work of ministry**, for the **edifying of the body of Christ**" (Ephesians 4:12).

What does the church experience when it is equipped and does ministry?
"Till we all come to the **unity of the faith** and of the knowledge of the Son of God, to a perfect man, to the measure of the stature of the fullness of Christ" (Ephesians 4:13).

What should the church do for its own members?
"Peter was therefore kept in prison, but constant **prayer was offered** to God for him **by the church**" (Acts 12:5).

How does Jesus feel about His church?
"Husbands, love your wives, just as **Christ** also **loved the church** and gave Himself for her" (Ephesians 5:25).

What is Jesus trying to do to His church?
"That He might **sanctify** and **cleanse her** with the **washing of water by the word**, that He might present her to Himself a glorious church, **not having spot or wrinkle** or any such thing, but that **she should be holy** and **without blemish**" (Ephesians 5:26, 27).

"If any believing man or woman has widows, let them relieve them, and do not let the church be burdened, **that it may relieve those who are really widows**" (1 Timothy 5:16).

Who is the head of the church?
" For the husband is head of the wife, as also **Christ is head of the church**; and He is the Savior of the body" (Ephesians 5:23).

WATCH

visit **answrs.co/search** to watch

In Search of the Church | 58:30

key elements of God's final church, sometimes referred to as the "remnant" (Revelation 12:17). That word, "remnant," appears in the book of Revelation, which, after depicting the history of persecution from the time of Jesus up to the end, describes God's faithful church like this: "And the dragon was wroth with the woman, and went to make war with the remnant of her seed, which keep the commandments of God, and have the testimony of Jesus Christ" (Revelation 12:17, KJV).

A few chapters later, in the context of the last days of Earth's history, a time of persecution and false worship, God's church is depicted like this: "Here is the patience of the saints: here are they that keep the commandments of God, and the faith of Jesus" (Revelation 14:12, KJV).

Both texts together show at least two overt identifying marks of those who comprise God's final church: they have the "faith of Jesus," that is, Jesus is central to their faith, and they "keep the commandments of God," which means all Ten Commandments. And, as we have seen (chapter 15), this would include the fourth commandment: the seventh-day Sabbath.

The Church

Sure, it's easy to be down on organized religion. No one knows the problems with organized religion better than God. Nevertheless, God also knows that humans cannot function very well alone. There's no such thing as a "one-man (or one-woman) church." Instead, with "Christ ... the head of the church" (Ephesians 5:23), He has created a community of life-minded believers, a fellowship of imperfect people who love God and who love each other and who want to share that love with a world that knows so much bigotry, hate, and suffering.

From that perspective, then, might not even a none admit that "organized religion," whatever its foibles, isn't so bad, after all?

READ MORE + SHARE THIS TOPIC
Visit **www.glowonline.org/answer/saturday** to read more about what you just read here. You can also share it on social media.

Why I go to Church on Saturday

7

14

Giving Light to Our World

Being confident of this very thing, that He who has begun a good work in you will *Complete* it until the day of Jesus Christ

Philippians 1:6

20

HEALTH

That You Prosper and Be in Health

A common theme in many religions is the idea that the soul, that is, the spiritual side of humanity, is good, as opposed to the body, the flesh, which is bad. This idea was seen in the writings of the philosopher Plato. In one scene, his teacher, Socrates, was about to die. As his followers were talking about his burial, Socrates said that they could bury him only "if you can catch me and I do not get away from you." The idea being that his soul, his immaterial soul, the good part of him, would fly away at death.

Nice story, but it doesn't fit with the biblical conception of our physical bodies.

Jesus, the Healer

If one reads the four Gospels, it becomes very clear that besides teaching, preaching, and ministering, Jesus of Nazareth did a lot of healing.

"And large crowds came to Him, bringing with them those who were lame, crippled, blind, mute, and many others, and they laid them down at His feet; and He healed them" (Matthew 15:30, NASB).

"While the sun was setting, all those who had any who were sick with various diseases brought them to Him; and laying His hands on each one of them, He was healing them" (Luke 4:40, NASB).

"One day He was teaching; and there were some Pharisees and teachers of the law sitting there, who had come from every village of Galilee and Judea and from Jerusalem; and the power of the Lord was present for Him to perform healing" (Luke 5:17, NASB).

And that's because, contrary to popular thought (even among some Christians), the human body is good, a creation of God, and we are to take the best care of it that we can.

Very Good

And no wonder: from the beginning, God blessed the created world. Though each day of creation was deemed "good," (Genesis 1:4, 10, 12, 18, 21, 25), after God finished making Adam and Eve, He declared the creation "very good" (Genesis 1:31). Nothing in the Bible makes any kind of moral separation between the body and soul, in the sense of the body, the flesh, being bad, and the soul, the spiritual, being good. Abuse of the body, abuse of the physical, is deemed bad, yes, but the physical, simply

WATCH visit **answrs.co/living** to watch *Living Life to the Fullest* | 58:30

visit **answrs.co/health** to watch a short video about what the Bible teaches about health | 2:28

Q&A FROM THE BIBLE

Does God care about our physical health as much as our spiritual health?
"Beloved, I pray that you may prosper in all things and **be in health, just as your soul prospers**" (3 John 2).

What is one way to improve our health?
"Do not be wise in your own eyes; fear the LORD and **depart from evil**. It will be **health** to your flesh, and strength to your bones" (Proverbs 3:7,8).

What kind of life does following God's principles give us?
"The thief does not come except to steal, and to kill, and to destroy. I have come that they **may have life**, and that they may **have it more abundantly**" (John 10:10).

Does God care about what we eat or drink?
"Therefore, whether you **eat or drink**, or whatever you do, **do all to the glory of God**" (1 Corinthians 10:31).

What was God's original diet for man when He created us?
"And God said, 'See, I have given you every **herb** that yields seed which is on the face of all the earth, and every tree whose **fruit** yields seed; to you it shall be for **food**." (Genesis 1:29).

Does God clearly outline which animals we can and should not eat?
"These **you may eat** of all that are **in the water**: whatever in the water has **fins and scales**, whether in the seas or in the rivers—that you may eat" (Leviticus 11:9).

"You may eat any animal that has a **divided hoof and that chews the cud**. There are some that only chew the cud or only have a divided hoof, but you must not eat them… And the pig, though it has a divided hoof, does not chew the cud; it is **unclean for you**. You must not eat their meat or touch their carcasses; they are unclean for you" (Leviticus 11:3-8, NIV).

What does God say about alcohol?
"**Wine is a mocker, strong drink is a brawler**, and whoever is led astray by it is not wise" (Proverbs 20:1).

What effect does drinking alcohol have on those who drink it?
"But they also have **erred** through **wine**, and through intoxicating drink are **out of the way**; the priest and the prophet have **erred** through intoxicating drink, they are swallowed up by wine, they are out of the way through intoxicating drink; they **err** in vision, they **stumble in judgment**" (Isaiah 28:7).

What should we not with wine aside from drinking it?
"**Do not look** on the wine when it is red, when it sparkles in the cup, when it swirls around smoothly; At the last it bites like a serpent, and stings like a viper. Your eyes will see strange things, and your heart will utter perverse things" (Proverbs 23:31-33).

"**Woe** to him who **gives drink to his neighbor**, pressing him to your bottle, even to make him drunk, that you may look on his nakedness!" (Habakkuk 2:15).

Why does God give us specific commandments?
"And the LORD commanded us to observe all these statutes, to fear the LORD our God, **for our good always**, that He might preserve us alive, as it is this day" (Deuteronomy 6:24).

What promise does God give us if we obey His commandments?
"If you diligently heed the voice of the LORD your God and do what is right in His sight, give ear to His commandments and keep all His statutes, I will put **none of the diseases** on you which I have **brought on the Egyptians**. For I am the LORD who heals you" (Exodus 15:26).

because it is physical, is not condemned.

Though the immediate context is sexual immorality, Paul writes, "Or do you not know that your body is the temple of the Holy Spirit who is in you, whom you have from God, and you are not your own?" (1 Corinthians 6:19). That's why, as Christians, as believers in the Bible, we are to take care of our physical health. Our bodies are gifts from God; they are who we are, and to abuse them is to abuse God's creation, a "temple of the Holy Spirit."

There are two main ways that we can take care of our bodies.

Diet and Exercise

In Eden, even before sin, diet and exercise were part of the original regimen for Adam and Eve. Their diet (Genesis 2:9) was plant-based; flesh eating didn't come in until much later, after the Flood (Genesis 9:1-5), probably because so much of the original vegetation had been destroyed.

How fascinating, too, that modern science gives powerful, almost overwhelming, evidence about the health advantages of a plant-based diet. That is, science shows that the diet that humans had been first given is optimal, the diet depicted in Scripture as the original one.

Second, the Bible says: "Then the LORD God took the man and put him in the garden of Eden to tend and keep it" (Genesis 2:15). As anyone who has ever worked in a garden knows, "to tend and keep" a garden can be very good exercise.

Modern science shows, too, the great benefits of exercise. Who hasn't heard from their doctor:

Q&A: Health

WATCH

visit **answrs.co/drunk** to watch a video answering questions including *Is it ok to drink a little alcohol, as long as you don't get drunk?* and *Did God know that people would live shorter lives after eating meat?*

LISTEN IN

visit **answrs.co/healthy** to listen to a presentation that goes along with what you're reading in this chapter.

exercise, exercise, exercise? Both physically and mentally, exercise is good for us.

New Bodies

Of course, we live in fallen world, one destined for destruction before being re-created (see chapters 16-17). In this new world we will enjoy new and incorruptible bodies. "For this corruptible must put on incorruption, and this mortal must put on immortality" (1 Corinthians 15:53).

Until then, we need to take as good care as we can of the bodies that we have now. As the apostle John wrote: "Beloved, I pray that you may prosper in all things and be in health, just as your soul prospers" (3 John 2).

steps to health

Giving Light to Our World

READ MORE + SHARE THIS TOPIC

Visit **www.glowonline.org/answer/health** to read more about what you just read here. You can also share it on social media.

21

FINANCES

Everyone knows this Bible text: "Money is the root of all evil." Only problem? It's not in the Bible. "For the love of money is a root of all kinds of evil" (1 Timothy 6:10)–that is in the Bible. Being rich, being wealthy, is not sinful; idolizing wealth and riches–that is. And there's a big difference between the two.

What, then, does the Bible teach about money and wealth?

The Bible and Money

A lot, actually. Some estimate that more than 2500 verses refer to money–many more, for instance, than verses where Jesus talked about love, death, or His Second Coming. Perhaps the gist of the biblical message about money could be expressed by two verses: "For what profit is it to a man if he gains the whole world, and loses his own soul? Or what will a man give in exchange for his soul?" (Matthew 16:26). And: "No one can serve two masters; for either he will hate the one and love the other, or else he will be loyal to the one and despise the other. You cannot serve God and mammon" (Matthew 6:24).

Both verses present an either/or situation: either your soul or the world, either God or mammon. In other words, if you are not careful, money–oops, the love of money–can lead to your destruction.

Tithes and Offerings

That's why the Lord has built in the Word a great protection for His people regarding money: tithes and offerings. Just as we give one-seventh of our time to God, we given one-tenth of our wealth to Him, as well, even though He owns it all anyway. "The earth is the LORD'S, and all its fullness" (Psalm 24:1). This is a truth we must never forget.

To help us remember, God has instituted tithes and offering. Abraham gave Melchizedek tithe (Genesis 14:20); there was an elaborate system of tithe and offering in ancient Israel (Deuteronomy 14:22; Malachi 3:10); and tithing existed in New Testament times as well (Matthew 23:23).

Your Money Where Your Mouth Is

It's not that God Himself needs the money. He doesn't. We need to tithe

WATCH visit **answrs.co/finances** to watch a short video about finances | 2:17

visit **answrs.co/tithe** to watch a video answering questions including *Is tithing mandatory?*

visit **answrs.co/money** to watch the program *Money, Money, Money* | 28:29

Q&A FROM THE BIBLE

Who gives us the power to gather wealth?
"And you shall remember the LORD your God, for **it is He who gives you power to get wealth**, that He may establish His covenant which He swore to your fathers, as it is this day" (Deuteronomy 8:18).

What is the root of all kinds of evil?
"For the **love of money** is a root of all kinds of evil, for which some have strayed from the faith in their greediness, and pierced themselves through with many sorrows" (1 Timothy 6:10).

So what does God provide for?
"And my God shall **supply all your needs** according to His riches in glory by Christ Jesus" (Philippians 4:19).

What should be our first priority before seeking to supply our material needs?
"Therefore do not worry, saying, 'What shall we eat?' or 'What shall we drink?' or 'What shall we wear?' For after all these things the Gentiles seek. For your heavenly Father knows that you need all these things. But **seek first** the kingdom of God and His righteousness, and all these things shall be **added to you**" (Matthew 6:31-33).

How should we not acquire our finances?
"A faithful man will abound with blessings, but he who **hastens to be rich** will not go unpunished" (Proverbs 28:20).

"Getting treasures by a **lying tongue** is the fleeting fantasy of those who seek death" (Proverbs 21:6).

"Wealth **gained by dishonesty** will be **diminished**, but he who gathers by labor will increase" (Proverbs 13:11).

What does God ask of us to do with our money to show we truly believe it comes from Him and that we trust in Him?
"And of all that You give me I will surely give **a tenth** to You" (Genesis 28:22).

Is it wrong not to pay our tithe, which is a tenth of what we earn, or our offerings to God?
"Will a man rob God? Yet **you have robbed Me**! But you say, 'In what way have we robbed You?' In **tithes and offerings**" (Malachi 3:8).

because, as we do, we acknowledge our dependence upon God. Tithing is an act of faith, an act of worship. If you are going to hand over at least 10 percent of your hard-earned money to God—you have to really trust in Him. And every act of faith only strengthens that faith and helps you protect yourself against greed, hoarding, and all the potential evils that come from the human fascination with money.

Anyone can say that they love God. But, by the paying of tithe and offering, you are, in a real sense, putting "your money where your mouth is." And though that phrase isn't in the Bible, when you pay tithes and offerings, "putting your money where your mouth is" is exactly what you are doing.

LISTEN IN visit **answrs.co/steward** to listen to a presentation that goes along with what you're reading in this chapter.

GROWING IN CHRIST

22

Two men were debating morality. One man insisted that morals were relative, cultural, contingent, depending only on where one lived and one's personal preferences. The other believed that morality came from God above, and in response to his opponent, said, "Kind sir, in one culture they teach you to love your neighbor, in the other to eat them. Which do you prefer?"

A New Life

Most would agree that they would prefer to live in a society where everyone loved their neighbors (as opposed to eating them). However, as many people know, it's easier to talk about loving others than to actually do it.

The good news of the gospel, however, is that God doesn't just tell us to love our neighbors, or even our enemies–as Jesus said, "But now I tell you: Love your enemies and pray for those who persecute you" (Matthew 5:44, GNT)–but we are promised power from Him to become new people in Jesus, people enabled to do the things that He asks of us.

Look at the following quotes, promises actually, from God:

"Therefore, if anyone is in Christ, he is a new creation; old things have passed away; behold, all things have become new" (2 Corinthians 5:17).

"Being confident of this very thing, that he which hath begun a good work in you will perform it until the day of Jesus Christ" (Philippians 1:6, KJV).

"A new heart also will I give you, and a new spirit will I put within you: and I will take away the stony heart out of your flesh, and I will give you a heart of flesh" (Ezekiel 36:26, KJV).

"I have been crucified with Christ; it is no longer I who live, but Christ lives in me; and the life which I now live in the flesh I live by faith in the Son of God, who loved me and gave Himself for me" (Galatians 2:20).

From Death to Life

In many ways, the Christian life begins in death. When we have a conversion experience, we are "born again" (John 3:3). That is, we first die to self, die to our sinful and selfish ways, and begin a new existence in Christ. At some point, we make a conscious choice to give ourselves to Christ, to seek to follow Him, and then the old person dies and we are new people in Christ Jesus.

WATCH visit **answrs.co/ growing** to see a short video on growing in Christ | 2:41

"Know ye not, that so many of us as were baptized into Jesus Christ were baptized into his death? Therefore we are buried with him by baptism into death: that like as Christ was raised up from the dead by the glory of the Father, even so we also should walk in newness of life" (Romans 6:3-4, KJV).

Baptism symbolizes the new person that we become. We go under the water, which represents not only Christ's death for us, but our death to our old sinful self. And, then, when we come up out of the water, that represents not only Christ's resurrection from the dead but our new life in Jesus Christ, a life of faith and obedience to Him.

The Holy Spirit

As we have saw in chapter 5, the Holy Spirit does the work of God in our lives, for He is God. Just as He has drawn us to Christ, He now works in us after we have come to Christ. It is the power of the Holy Spirit working in us who changes us into the image of Christ (Galatians 4:19). The Holy Spirit works in us, transforming us into sons and daughters of God, new people who live in the freedom of knowing that they have been reconciled to God by the death of Jesus in their behalf.

Though the moment that we accept Christ, we stand forgiven in Him, accepted by God as if we have never sinned, our Christian journey at that

LISTEN IN visit **answrs.co/grace** to listen to a presentation that goes along with what you're reading in this chapter.

Q&A FROM THE BIBLE

What is man's natural condition?
"As it is written: 'There is **none righteous**, no, not one; there is **none who understands**; there is **none who seeks after God**" (Romans 3:10, 11).

"Because the **carnal mind** is enmity against God; for it is not subject to the law of God, nor indeed can be" (Romans 8:7).

What is one object that God uses to illustrate the Christian experience?
"He shall be **like a tree** planted by the rivers of water, that **brings forth its fruit in its season**, whose leaf also shall not wither; and whatever he does shall prosper" (Psalm 1:4).

What does God ask of us to do as Christians?
"But **grow** in the grace and knowledge of our Lord and Savior Jesus Christ" (2 Peter 3:18).

How does a Christian grow in grace?
"Grace and peace be **multiplied** to you in the **knowledge of God** and of Jesus our Lord" (2 Peter 1:2).

Where does a knowledge of God come from?
"Apply your heart to instruction, and your ears to **words of knowledge**" (Proverbs 23:12).

"For the **LORD gives** wisdom; from His **mouth** come **knowledge** and understanding" (Proverbs 2:6).

What is the main point of the Bible that I should focus on in my studies?
"You search the Scriptures, for in them you think you have eternal life; and these are they which testify of **Me** [Jesus]" (John 5:39).

"**Jesus** said to him, 'I am the way, the truth, and the life. No one comes to the Father **except through Me**'" (John 14:6).

moment has only just begun. We then, by faith, by grace, sometimes stumbling, sometimes falling, and often falling short of what we know we could and should be, we are not rejected by God. Instead, we repent, and through the power of the Holy Spirit, we begin to reject the works of flesh, "adultery, fornication, uncleanness, lewdness, idolatry, sorcery, hatred, contentions, jealousies, outbursts of wrath, selfish ambitions, dissensions, heresies, envy, murders, drunkenness, revelries" (Galatians 5:19-21). Instead, we reflect the fruit of the Spirit: "love, joy, peace, longsuffering, kindness, goodness, faithfulness, gentleness, self-control" (Galatians 5:22, 23).

The Life of Faith

The Christian life, like all human life, is filled with drama, trial, disappointments, and hurt. As Paul himself wrote: "We must through many tribulations enter the kingdom of God" (Acts 14:22). But we can know that we are not alone in our

WATCH

visit **answrs.co/pray** to watch a video answering questions including
How should I pray?
Can you explain grace to me? and
Do I have to be perfect in order to be saved?

"And this is eternal life, that **they may know You**, the only true God, and Jesus Christ whom You have sent" (John 17:3).

What should I do with the knowledge of God that I gain from reading the Word of God?
"This Book of the Law shall not depart from your mouth, but you shall **meditate** in it **day and night**, that you may observe to do according to all that is written in it. For then you will make your way prosperous, and then you will have good success" (Joshua 1:8).

What experience will I have if I spend time daily in God's Word reading and thinking about it?
"Having been **born again**, not of corruptible seed but incorruptible, **through the word of God** which lives and abides forever" (1 Peter 1:23).

What does it mean to be born again?
"Therefore, if anyone is in Christ, he is a **new creation**; **old things** have **passed away**; behold, **all things have become new**" (2 Corinthians 5:17).

"Since you have **purified your souls** in **obeying the truth** through the Spirit in sincere love of the brethren, **love one another** fervently with a **pure heart**, having been born again (1 Peter 1:22, 23).

What "fruits" will grow in my life as I daily grow through Christ into a new creature?
"But the **fruit of the Spirit** is love, joy, peace, longsuffering, kindness, goodness, faithfulness, gentleness, self-control" (Galatians 5:22, 23).

How is it that by daily reading and thinking about the Word of God I will be changed?
"For **as he thinks** in his heart, **so is he**" (Proverbs 23:7).

Can I do this work on my own?
"Can the Ethiopian change his skin or the leopard its spots? Then may you also do good

who are accustomed to do evil" (Jeremiah 13:23).

Who then ultimately changes my heart as I spend time in the Word of God?
"This is the covenant that I will make with them after those days, **says the LORD**: I will put My laws into their **hearts**, and in their **minds** I will write them" (Hebrews 10:16).

What happens if we choose to not gain a knowledge of God or to be born again?
"Jesus answered and said to him, "Most assuredly, I say to you, unless one is born again, he **cannot see the kingdom of God**" (John 3:3).

"**Not everyone** who says to Me, 'Lord, Lord,' **shall enter** the kingdom of heaven, but he who does the will of My Father in heaven. Many will say to Me in that day, "Lord, Lord, have we not prophesied in Your name, cast out demons in Your name, and done many wonders in Your name?' And then I will declare to them, "**I never knew you**; depart from Me, you who practice lawlessness!'" (Matthew 27:21-23).

What advice does Jesus give to His believers?
"**Watch and pray**, lest you enter into temptation. The spirit indeed is willing, but the flesh is weak" (Matthew 26:41).

How often should we pray?
"Pray **without ceasing**" (1 Thessalonians 5:7).

Can we be confident that God hears and desires to answer our prayers?
"Now this is the **confidence** that we have in Him, that if we **ask anything** according to **His will, He hears us**. And if we know that He hears us, whatever we ask, we know that we have the petitions that we have asked of Him" (1 John 5:14,15).

tribulations. The presence and power of our God is with us, offering strength, consolation, and hope. We can know, not that all things are good, but that "all things work together for good to those who love God, to those who are the called according to His purpose" (Romans 8:28).

Through a life of prayer (us talking to God), Bible study (God talking to us), and good works (God working through us to minister to others), we will grow and mature in our Christian faith, always aware of our inherent sinfulness and our constant need of Christ, His grace, His power, and His promises.

The reality of the cross, of what it cost God to save us, that it was nothing short of the self-sacrifice of God Himself on the cross, should keep us humble, teachable, and faithful. Knowing that the God who created all that was created, the entire cosmos, "shrank down" and became a human baby, lived in perfect obedience to the Father, and then, according to "His own purpose and grace which was given to us in Christ Jesus before time began" (2 Timothy 1:9) offered Himself as a divine-human sacrifice for us, should ever keep us seeking to live in faithful submission to Him and to His will.

As we do that, God will, as Scripture says, work "in you both to will and to do for His good pleasure" (Philippians 2:13). This is the life of faith and of growing in grace—simply God working His will and good pleasure in us.

Talking WITH GOD

Giving Light to Our World

READ MORE + SHARE THIS TOPIC
Visit **www.glowonline.org/answer/prayer** to read more about what you just read here. You can also share it on social media.

23

MARRIAGE & FAMILY

Family Affairs

Years ago, a German poet wanted to leave money to whoever married his widow because, he said, he would know that "at least one person would mourn my death."

In his autobiography, American president Calvin Coolidge mentioned his wife only once, writing: "My wife died today."

Ouch! These are two sad commentaries on what was created to be one of humanity's greatest blessing from God: marriage and the family.

From Praise to Blame

God originally created two genders, "male and female He created them" (Genesis 1:27), a husband and wife. "Therefore a man shall leave his father and mother and be joined to his wife, and they shall become one flesh" (Genesis 2:24).

Of course, after sin, everything was damaged, and perhaps nothing took a greater hit than marriage and the family. The first time Scripture has Adam mention his wife, he utters some wonderful poetic words about her (Genesis 2:23); the next time he mentions her, however, is after they sinned, and his words about her are words of blame: "The woman whom You gave to be with me, she gave me of the tree, and I ate" (Genesis 3:12).

From praise to blame—and things went downhill from there, not just for Adam and Eve, but for all humanity as well.

Marriage and Family

Nevertheless, the gospel, as we have seen, is about restoration, about bringing things back to what they originally were. Though this process will not be completed until after the Second Coming, we can—through God's grace—begin the process of restoration now. And nowhere is this change, this restoration, more important than in the home and the family.

Today, yes, there are all sorts of "marriages," all sorts of "families," and we cannot judge those in such relationships. Many people, such as the children, had no more choice in choosing their family and home than any of us did ours.

However, the original model was one man and one woman in a perpetual union of faithfulness and love to each other—and only to each other. Yes, we also find polygamy in the Bible,

Q&A: Marriage & Family

WATCH visit **answrs.co/marriage** to watch a short video about marriage in the Bible | 2:16

visit **answrs.co/divorce** to watch a video answering questions including *When is it OK to get a divorce?*

visit **answrs.co/living** to watch the program *Living Life to the Fullest* | 58:30

even by men deemed faithful to God. But that doesn't mean God approved. In many of the stories, these relationships brought suffering and pain upon both the parents and children.

LISTEN IN

visit **answrs.co/family** to listen to a presentation that goes along with this chapter.

A Loving Home

It's true, too, unfortunately, that many "traditional" homes don't model God's plan for family life. Sexual, verbal, or physical abuse, infidelity, selfishness, bullying—a host of aberrations can make what was supposed to be the most secure, loving, and safe place be anything but. None of this was in God's plan, and only in hearts that are

Q&A FROM THE BIBLE

When was marriage first instituted?
"And the LORD God caused a deep sleep to fall on Adam, and he slept; and He took one of his ribs, and closed up the flesh in its place. Then the rib which the LORD God had taken from man **He made into a woman**, and **He brought her to the man**" (Genesis 2:21, 22).

Why did God give us marriage?
"And the LORD God said, 'It is **not good that man should be alone**; I will make him a helper comparable to him'" (Genesis 2:18).

How many people should we marry?
"Therefore **a man** shall leave his father and mother and be joined to **his wife**, and they shall become **one flesh**" (Genesis 2:24).

Who is it that join husband and wife together when they are married?
"So then, they are no longer two but one flesh. Therefore what **God has joined together**, let not man separate" (Matthew 19:6).

Since God has joined them together how does He feel about divorce?
"For the LORD God of Israel says that **He hates divorce**" (Malachi 2:6).

When is the only time divorce is an option?
"And I say to you, whoever divorces his wife, **except for sexual immorality**, and marries another, commits adultery; and whoever marries her who is divorced commits adultery" (Matthew 19:9).

When asked why God allowed divorce in Moses' time, what was Jesus' response?
"He said to them, 'Moses, because of the **hardness of your hearts**, permitted you to divorce your wives, but **from the beginning it was not so**'" (Matthew 19:8).

How should the husband and wife relate to each other?
"The heart of her husband **safely trusts her**" (Proverbs 31:11).

"Her husband also, and **he praises her**" (Proverbs 31:28).

"Husbands, **love your wives** and **do not be bitter** toward them" (Colossians 3:19).

"But he who is married cares about the things of the world—**how he may please his wife** … But she who is married cares about the things of the world—**how she may please her husband**" (1 Corinthians 7:33, 34).

"Be kindly affectionate to one another with brotherly love, in honor **giving preference to one another**" (Romans 12:10).

How should husband and wife relate to each others mistakes?
"And above all things have fervent love for one

now surrendered to the Lord in love for Him and for each other can healing come.

Whatever your home life, whatever your mistakes, or the mistakes of others, the Lord knows about it all. In fact, for any who come in faith, He is willing to forgive, to heal, and to restore our families, now and for eternity.

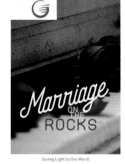

READ MORE + SHARE THIS TOPIC

Visit **www.glowonline.org/answer/marriage** to read more about what you just read here. You can also share it on social media.

another, for '**love will cover a multitude of sins**'" (1 Peter 4:8).

What should a husband and wife not allow if they are angry with each other?
"Be angry, and do not sin: **do not let the sun go down on your wrath** … and be kind to one another, tenderhearted, **forgiving one another**, even as God in Christ forgave you" (Ephesians 4:26, 32).

In order to have the type of experience God intends for married couples, what needs to be at the center of their relationship?
"Unless **the LORD** builds the house, they labor in vain who build it" (Psalm 127:1).

What does God require of our children?
"**Honor your father and your mother**, that your days may be long upon the land which the LORD your God is giving you" (Exodus 20:12).

What does God require of parents?
"And these words which I command you today shall be in your heart. **You shall teach** them **diligently to your children**, and shall **talk of them** when you sit in your house, when you walk by the way, when you lie down, and when you rise up" (Deuteronomy 6:6, 7).

Should parents correct or discipline their children?
"**Correct your son**, and he will give you rest; Yes, he will give delight to your soul" (Proverbs 29:17).

What is the result if you neglect this duty?
"The rod and rebuke give wisdom, but a **child left to himself brings shame** to his mother" (Proverbs 29:15).

Doesn't it mean I don't love my child if I discipline them?
"He who spares his rod hates his son, but **he who loves him disciplines** him promptly" (Proverbs 13:24).

When raising children what should parents be careful not to do?
"And you, fathers, **do not provoke your children to wrath**, but bring them up in the training and admonition of the Lord" (Ephesians 6:4).

"Fathers, **do not embitter** your children, or they will become discouraged" (Colossians 3:21, NIV).

What promise does God give to parents?
"Train up a child in the way he should go, and when he is old **he will not depart from it**" (Proverbs 22:6).

What does Biblical love look like?
"Love is **patient**, love is **kind**. It does not envy, it does not boast, it is not proud. It does not dishonor others, it is not self-seeking, it is not easily angered, it keeps no record of wrongs. Love does not delight in evil but **rejoices with the truth**. It always **protects**, always **trusts**, always **hopes**, always **perseveres**" (1 Corinthians 13:4-7, NIV).

CONCLUSION

Is the Universe Friendly?

We began *The Answer Book* with a quote, the profundity of which might have been lost amid the colloquiality of its expression: "Seems like we're just set down here, and don't nobody know why." We, indeed, have been "set down here"; whether "don't nobody know why"—well, that clause can be debated.

This quote, though, leads to another—one that we'd like to end with: "Is the universe friendly?

In other words, the universe we have been "set down" in—is it friendly to us? For all its simplicity (and better grammar than the first quote), this question is profound, because its answer contains implications for intelligent, moral beings, like us, who happen to find ourselves stuck in this universe.

Besides, if the universe—with its black holes, mind-numbing distances, exploding stars, and colliding galaxies—had malevolent designs on us poor little earthlings here, it doesn't seem that there's much we could do about it. Or, perhaps, as modern thought says, the universe is indifferent to us; we are mere cosmic debris, happenstance creations who through chance chemical reactions on a blob of cooling lava billions of years ago arose and will eventually revert back to those same chemicals. And that will be it. End of story.

Though one could argue that scenario is better than a universe with malevolent designs on us, it still paints a bleak picture.

"Oh, you wretches who feel all this," wrote German poet Fredrich Hölderlin, "who, even as I, cannot allow yourselves to speak of man's being here for a purpose, who, even as I, are so utterly in the clutch of the Nothing that governs us, so profoundly aware that we are born for nothing, that we love a nothing, believe in nothing, work ourselves to death for nothing only that little by little we may pass over into nothing—how can I help it if your knees collapse when you think of it seriously?"

A bit of a bummer, yes, but understandable still.

The Love of God

On the other hand, we have taken a completely different approach. Better than the universe being friendly, it posits that the God who created the universe, and who upholds it—He is not just "friendly" but so full of self-sacrificing love for us, we poor earthlings "just set down here," that He died on the cross for us, the only way to save us from the fate that would otherwise await us: going back to the utter nothingness out from which we first came.

Wrote the apostle Paul about the love of God for us, as revealed in Christ Jesus: "Let this mind be in you which was also in Christ Jesus, who, being in the form of God, did not consider it robbery to be equal with God, but made Himself of no reputation, taking the form of a bondservant, and coming in the likeness of men. And being found in appearance as a man, He humbled Himself and became obedient to the point of death, even the death of the cross" (Philippians 2:5-8).

Thus, even with all that we have looked at in this book, the teachings—on everything from prayer and the Sabbath, to death and the Second Coming—all important in their own right—the ultimate truth that trumps all others is that of Jesus on the cross, the One "equal with God" dying for us. Everything in *The Answer Book*—everything—ultimately comes back to the cross and the hope that it offers us amid a world that, in and of itself, offers us, at best, some good years of life (if we are fortunate) and then, always and inevitably, death. For us, as beings who can not only contemplate the idea of eternity but fear what it means to be left behind in it—what the earth offers us is nothing but the hope that death, which we hate so much, is our only out from the pain and turmoil that can so often dominate this life.

It's pretty bad when death, hateful death, is our only hope.

The Cross of Christ

But, as *The Answer Book* has shown, death is not the answer but the question that, itself, needs to be answered and solved. It was answered and solved, through the self-sacrifice of God Himself, in the person of Jesus, on the cross.

What is the cross? It's when the One whose power had created and upheld the unnumbered worlds through the vast realms of space, the Beloved of God, the Majesty of heaven—it's when He humbled Himself to uplift fallen man by taking upon Himself the punishment that was ours so we could have the eternal life that was His.

As one writer expressed how the redeemed throughout eternity will view the cross: "That the Maker of all worlds, the Arbiter of all destinies, should lay aside His glory and humiliate Himself from love to man will ever excite the wonder and adoration of the universe. As the nations of the saved look upon their Redeemer and behold the eternal glory of the Father shining in His countenance; as they behold His throne, which is from everlasting to everlasting, and know that His kingdom is to have no end, they break forth in rapturous song: 'Worthy, worthy is the Lamb that was slain, and hath redeemed us to God by His own most precious blood!'" (*Maranatha*, p.362).

And if, in some way, *The Answer Book* has helped you get even a glimpse of that glory, the eternal glory that will ever shine from the cross, the writing was worth it.

SCRIPTURE INDEX

TOPICAL INDEX

![It Is Written TV logo]

Now you can enjoy
It Is Written programs 24/7!

It Is Written's new TV channel has a great lineup of Christian programs for the whole family. From *It Is Written Classics* programs by founder George Vandeman to new episodes of *Line Upon Line* and *In The Word*, It Is Written TV offers thousands of hours to inspire and uplift.

You can watch It Is Written TV online anytime at **itiswritten.tv**.

Look for It Is Written programs on these devices:

IT IS WRITTEN
Classics
REMASTERED

LINE UPON LINE
NEW SERIES

In the Word
NEW SERIES

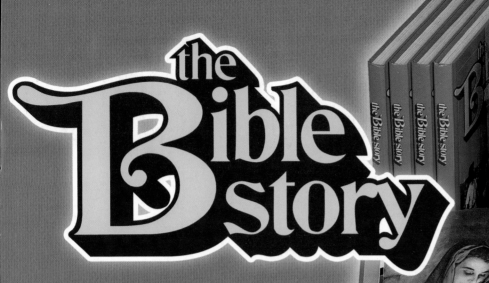